CHILDREN'S UNDERSTANDING OF SOCIAL INTERACTION

A Publication of
The Horace Mann-Lincoln Institute
Teachers College, Columbia University

CHILDREN'S UNDERSTANDING

OF SOCIAL INTERACTION

Dorothy Flapan

TEACHERS COLLEGE PRESS
Teachers College, Columbia University
New York, New York

Acknowledgments

This study was an independent part of a research project dealing with the development of children's and adolescents' awareness and perception of their own and others' feelings and motives. The project, directed by Dr. Arthur T. Jersild, was conducted under the auspices of the Horace Mann-Lincoln Institute of School Experimentation, Teachers College, Columbia University. Many people generously helped to make this particular study possible and to bring it to a conclusion.

More than thanks are due to Professor Jersild, who went far beyond any call of duty in giving of his time and of himself. During a close working association of more than four years, he offered criticism, encouragement and emotional support at times when they were most needed and consequently most beneficial. From the beginning of this research, he willingly offered help and wisdom through all the unanticipated crises. Throughout he has been a loyal friend just as much as a conscientious adviser.

Dr. Harold C. Ahlquist, Principal of the Hillside Elementary School, Hastings-on-Hudson, New York, gave access to the children who participated in this study and provided space and equipment, and the writer expresses warm thanks to him and to the children.

The writer is indebted to Professors Elizabeth P. Hagen, Joel R. Davitz, and Miriam Goldberg for their interest, suggestions and helpful advice; to Professor Howard Hunt who raised pertinent and challenging questions that led the writer to think about basic problems and to clarify some of her thoughts; and to Professor Rosedith Sitgreaves who, at a time when the writer was struggling with the problem of finding a meaningful way of presenting the findings, suggested an approach to the measurement of significance and a way of organizing the tables that enabled the whole study "to fall into place."

A very special word of appreciation is due to two "voluntary research assistants," Renne Flapan and Erica Flapan, who, at the ages of eight years and six years respectively, offered their opinions and criticisms during the preliminary phase of the study, when film-strips were being viewed and discarded and interview questions were being formulated, and then gave patient understanding, solace, and welcome diversion during the subsequent years that the study was being completed.

DOROTHY FLAPAN

Foreword

Dr. Flapan's study, reported here, is the most recent in a long series devoted to child development conducted through the Horace Mann-Lincoln Institute. The first study published by the Institute was Jersild's; others by Cunningham and Almy have appeared at regular intervals over a twenty-year period.

Like these others, Dr. Flapan's study innovates in method. The use of filmed episodes as the basis for these significant observations of children's social and emotional growth had not been tried when this study was undertaken. Methodologically, the study combines the virtues of the rigor of earlier studies and the warmth and flare that characterize many of the more recent reports, especially those that have been pointed at the general audience. Some well-known generalizations about children are supported by this study; it has certain features of its own. Dr. Flapan is personally occupied with the application of child development to the growth of children. Her commitment to the importance and reality of childhood is reflected repeatedly in this report, as it is in her professional conduct.

The members of the Horace Mann-Lincoln Institute will long remember the evening when Dr. Flapan showed the filmed episodes used in the study, and told us what the children had said about them. Research reports are often (sometimes necessarily) dry and impersonal. The warmth and directness of this study contrasted so sharply with most other research we had known that many of us were deeply stirred.

It is, indeed, a stirring study, if the reader will give himself to it. Dr. Flapan's colleagues of the Horace Mann-Lincoln Institute share her satisfaction in seeing it appear.

ARTHUR W. FOSHAY

Contents

1

Background of the Study

This is a study of children's ability to perceive or to make inferences about feelings, thoughts, and intentions, and of their ability to interpret or explain sequences of behavior that occur in interpersonal relationships. It is based on work with children at three age levels — six, nine, and twelve. It uses sound-motion pictures to represent, as closely as can be achieved, living person-to-person interactions that occur in everyday life.

The present investigation explores an area of cognition about which relatively little is known. There is a vast literature today dealing with the cognitive development of children and focusing on children's thinking in dealing with such concepts as number, space, and other impersonal topics. But inquiries into these topics do not tell us much concerning aspects of cognition that have an important role in interpersonal relationships.

This study raises several questions. What aspects of an episode of social interaction that they have witnessed do children spontaneously report about? In reporting their observations, to what extent do they speak in terms of overt actions and dialogues and to what extent do they make inferences about feelings, thoughts, and intentions? Do they give explanations for the interaction observed? And, if so, are their explanations based on an interpretation of the past actions or future goals of the "actors" in the situation? If their attention is directed to a specific aspect of an episode of interaction, what kinds of meaning do they "read" into what they have seen and heard? Does this change with age, as shown by comparisons between different age groups? Do older children offer types of comments that seldom or never occur with younger children and that might lead to the conclusion that there are developmental stages in this type of cognition?

Social scientists have used a variety of concepts to designate the process by which an individual understands social interaction — concepts such as social sensitivity, sympathetic introspection, taking the role of the other, empathy, social perception. Each of these concepts refers to a somewhat different aspect of the process by which social interaction is understood. Yet, on the whole, investigation of these processes has not been along developmental lines.

Related Studies

Though there is no body of systematic findings that throws light on the questions raised in the larger project of which this study was a part (for example, what are the characteristics of and developmental trends in children's awareness of their own and others' feelings, thoughts, and intentions?), much of the work that has been done in other areas of development can be related to the present study.

Piaget and his followers have offered the most comprehensive theoretical and empirical contributions in the study of various facets of cognitive development. The classic work of Piaget has centered largely on the nature of children's thinking in dealing with problems that are objective and impersonal in character, while the present study asks, not only how children perceive objective aspects of interpersonal interaction, but also what are the characteristics of their cognition when asked about subjective states that might be inferred from behavior.

Piaget regards development as a continuous process, but emphasizes stages of development. These stages not only denote that at a certain age most children function in a certain way, but also describe the sequences through which a child passes as he moves from a less to a more mature form of thinking. Although Piaget's work deals primarily with cognition as manifested by children's thinking about problems relating to quantity, size, space, and other impersonal, objective properties of natural phenomena, he has advanced one concept that has considerable relevance to the present investigation — the concept of egocentricity. In the area of language, Piaget described the development from "egocentric" language to "socialized" language.[1] In line with this he concluded that the older child is more capable of viewing situations from the standpoint of other persons, has a more genuine interchange of ideas in his discussions, and unlike the younger child,

---

[1] J. Piaget, *The language and thought of the child* (3rd ed.) (New York: Humanities Press, 1959).

is better able to communicate the workings of his thought processes.[2] He further stated that until the age of seven or eight the "egocentric factors of verbal expression . . . and of understanding itself, as well as the derivative factors (such as lack of order in the accounts given, juxtaposition, etc.) are too important to allow of any genuine understanding between children."[3] A question for the present study, therefore, was whether the young child's difficulty in disengaging himself from his own personal view of things when dealing with impersonal relationships also interferes with his ability to describe and interpret the thoughts and feelings that are involved in interpersonal relationships.

In considering the development of logical intelligence, Piaget[4] stated that children at the six- to seven-year level think largely in perceptual rather than conceptual terms, while at about the eleven- to twelve-year level the child's thought is less tied to the concrete and he is more capable of abstract reasoning. This raises the question of whether the young child, in talking about social interaction, also thinks largely in perceptual rather than conceptual terms.

In his discussion of moral development, Piaget[5] described older children as being able to judge the seriousness of an act in terms of the intentions of persons, whereas the younger children judge the act in terms of its physical consequences and in terms of literal rules. In the present study, the aim was not to get children to pass a moral judgment as to the goodness or badness of what others do, feel, or think, but to inquire into ways in which children describe and interpret others' experiences. Yet the question can be raised as to the relation between the ability to describe or interpret a manifestation of a feeling or an intention and the notions a child has as to the goodness or badness of what happened.

Piaget[6] also noted that six-year-olds, when repeating narrative stories or offering mechanical explanations, rarely speak in terms of causal relationships. He concluded that the child places more stress on the events themselves than on the "relations of time (order) or cause which unite them." Another question, then, is whether the child of six has a similar difficulty in applying the concept of causation to the observation of human behavior.

There are other aspects of cognitive development that might also

[2] J. Piaget, *Judgment and reasoning in the child* (New York: Harcourt, Brace, 1928), and *The language and thought of the child.*

[3] J. Piaget, *The language and thought of the child* (3rd ed.) (New York: Humanities Press, 1959), p. 125.

[4] B. Inhelder and J. Piaget, *The growth of logical thinking from childhood to adolescence* (New York: Basic Books, 1958).

[5] J. Piaget, *The moral judgment of the child* (Glencoe: Free Press, 1960).

[6] J. Piaget, *The language and thought of the child*, p. 125.

be related to the findings emerging in the present study. In his review of studies of children's thinking, Russell noted that the formation of concepts moves ". . . along a continuum from simple to complex, from concrete to abstract, from undifferentiated to differentiated, from discrete to organized, and from egocentric to social."[7] Along this same line, Ausubel summarized work in this area, stating:

> Cognitive development during childhood is characterized by an increasing ability to comprehend and manipulate verbal symbols and to employ abstract classificatory schemata. This trend has several major self-evident implications for perceptual and cognitive functions. First, . . . the anticipation of consequences and the pretesting of alternatives are facilitated. Second, the child becomes more responsive to abstract features of his environment, and in turn apprehends the world in more abstract and categorical terms than in terms of tangible, time-bound and particularized contexts.[8]

This raises the question of whether in children's thinking about social interaction there is also a development from the simple to the complex, the concrete to the abstract, the discrete to the organized.

Other work, in the area of children's perceptions, has indicated a development that is increasingly more schematic with age.[9] That is, with advancing age children structure their percepts along less literal lines and omit irrelevant details. In studies of intelligence generally, there appears to be a development from the specific to the general, and from the concrete to the abstract. Would the same trends appear in the aspect of cognitive development of interest in the present study? In talking about episodes of social interaction, would children, with age, report in less literal ways and omit irrelevant details?

Studies of social development have also indicated age trends. With age children show an increase in the ability to select the "best" action in a problem situation,[10] and in the ability to predict their own or their classmates' sociometric ratings.[11] With age they show an increase in

[7] D. H. Russell, *Children's thinking* (Boston: Ginn, 1956), p. 249.

[8] D. P. Ausubel, *Theory and problems of child development* (New York: Grune and Stratton, 1958).

[9] J. J. Gibson, "Social psychology and the psychology of perceptual learning," in M. Sherif and M. O. Wilson (eds.), *Group relations at the crossroads* (New York: Harper, 1958), pp. 120–38.

[10] Jui Ching Hsia, *A study of the sociability of elementary school children.* (Contributions to Education, No. 322 [New York: Bureau of Publications, Teachers College, Columbia Univ., 1928]); C. G. Gibbons and J. P. Porter, "Some aspects of social adaptability among adolescents," *J. Appl. Psychol.*, XXIII (1939), 508–20.

[11] D. P. Ausubel, "Socioempathy as a function of sociometric status in an adolescent group," *Human Relat.*, VIII (1955), 75–84; D. P. Ausubel & H. M. Schiff,

empathy[12] and an increase in sympathy.[13] In studies in which a still picture was presented, there was an age trend from perception of concrete, often unrelated details of a situation to a recognition of these concrete details as parts of some larger whole, and to an interpretation of them as symbols of subjective experience.[14] Burns and Cavey[15] found that younger nursery school children, three to five years, judged drawings in terms of what they themselves would feel in the situation rather than in terms of the cues presented, whereas older nursery school children, five to six years, apparently realized the children depicted in drawings were not experiencing the feelings the subject himself would feel in such a situation.

In separate studies, Gates[16] and Walton[17] found that the ability to identify the emotions portrayed by an actress in a photograph increased with age. Walton stated that the children's classification of emotions as pleasant or unpleasant agreed with the classification made by adults, but by fourth grade finer differences were being made between the reactions, and the "rough two-dimensional classification" had disappeared. Gollin[18] concluded that the use of inference in interpreting observed behavior is a relatively *late* developmental phenomenon. Yet Yarrow and Campbell[19] stated that even though older children tended to give more complex perceptual reports, they found relatively minor evidence of developmental trends and concluded that this may be a

---

"Some intrapersonal and interpersonal determinants of individual differences in socio-empathetic ability among adolescents," *J. Soc. Psychol.*, XLI (1955), 39–56; D. P. Ausubel, H. M. Schiff and E. B. Gasser, "A preliminary study of developmental trends in socioempathy: accuracy of perception of own and others' sociometric status," *Child Develpm.*, XXIII (1952), 111–28; R. V. Miller, "Social status and socioempathic differences," *Except. Child.*, XXIII (1956), 114–19; J. R. Davitz, "Social perception and sociometric choice of children," *J. Abnorm. Soc. Psychol.*, L (1955), 173–76.

[12] Rosalind F. Dymond, Anne S. Hughes, and Virginia L. Raabe, "Measurable changes in empathy with age," *J. Consult. Psychol.*, XVI (1952), 202–206.

[13] J. E. Bathurst, "A study of sympathy and resistance (negativism) among children," *Psychol. Bull.*, XXX (1933), 625–26; Lois Murphy, *Social behavior and child personality* (New York: Columbia Univ. Press, 1937).

[14] Elizabeth W. Amen, "Individual differences in apperceptive reaction: A study of the response of preschool children to pictures." *Genet. Psychol. Monogr.*, XXIII (1941), 319–85; F. J. Estvan & Elizabeth W. Estvan, *The child's world: His social perception* (New York: G. P. Putnam's, 1959).

[15] Neal Burns and Lorna Cavey, "Age differences in empathic ability among children," *Canad. J. Psychol.*, XI (1957), 227–30.

[16] Georgina Strickland Gates, "An experimental study of the growth of social perception," *J. Educ. Psychol.*, XIV (1923), 449–61.

[17] W. E. Walton, "Empathic responses in children," *Psychol. Monogr.*, XLVIII (1936), 40–67.

[18] E. S. Gollin, "Organizational characteristics of social judgment: A developmental investigation," *J. Pers.*, XXVI (1958), 139–54.

[19] Marian Radke-Yarrow & J. D. Campbell, "Person perception in children," *Merrill-Palmer Quarterly*, IX (1963), 57–72.

reflection of the early development of sensitivities to interpersonal relations.

Winch[20] found that the capacity to observe and report grew rapidly from age three to about six or seven and then seemed to suffer a setback. He questioned, however, whether there was a natural decline of interest and capacity, or whether the setback in scores was due to the fact that the eight- to thirteen-year-old group wrote their answers while the younger group was individually interviewed.

Again the question may be raised as to whether a similar age trend appears in the specific aspect of cognition here being studied.

Assessment Strategy

An essential preliminary task in the present study was to find a way of presenting social interaction in a manner that would elicit pertinent information. Earlier studies dealing more directly with social perception, empathy, or interpretation of expressive reactions depended largely on children's responses to still pictures, verbally presented situations, projective materials, or sociometric techniques.

In several studies the child was given something static to look at, such as a line drawing, a more complete drawing, or a photograph, and then was questioned about the picture.[21] What had he seen? What was the picture about? What story did the picture tell? What was the lady feeling, or thinking about, or doing? In a somewhat different approach, Burns and Cavey[22] presented nursery school children with four still pictures showing a birthday party scene, the same scene with a child with a frown, a scene showing a doctor with a long needle, the same scene with a child with a smile on his face. For the "empty" scenes (i.e., scenes without a child) the children were asked, "How would you feel in this situation?" and for the other two scenes the children were asked, "How does he (she) feel?"

In a study by Gollin[23] a silent movie was used, presenting the same boy in four scenes, two in which he was "good" and two in which he was "bad." Here the children were to write "what you think of this boy and the things you saw him do."

Other studies used the procedure of telling the child a story or presenting him with a written description of a situation and then asking

[20] W. H. Winch, "Children's perceptions," *Educ. Psychol. Monogr.*, No. 12 (Baltimore: Warwick and York, 1914).

[21] W. H. Winch, *op. cit.*; Elizabeth W. Amen, *op. cit.*; F. J. Estvan & Elizabeth W. Estvan, *op. cit.*; Georgina Strickland Gates, *op. cit.*

[22] Neal Burns & Lorna Cavey, *op. cit.*

[23] E. S. Gollin, *op. cit.*

him to imagine himself in similar circumstances or to imagine the feelings and thoughts of the characters in the story.[24] Written descriptions of situations have also been used in studies where the child has been required to choose the best of four alternative courses of action.[25] In addition, Ojemann and his associates[26] used written descriptions in a "Problems Situations Test," where instances of misbehavior or deficiency of children were presented to the subject, who was to deal with these from the point of view of an authority figure by selecting from multiple-choice alternatives; and in a "Causal Test," where descriptions of behavior were presented to the subject, who was to answer true-false items concerned with motivation.

Other studies can be grouped together as studies in which the child's response or performance was based on some previous experiences or interactions with peers rather than on something presented directly by the experimenter. Harris[27] used a series of line drawings of children in varying situations, each illustrating a particular behavior or personality trait, and asked kindergarten children to tell who at school did this and what the child was doing. Other investigators asked children to predict the sociometric ratings given to them by their classmates and to predict the sociometric standing of each of their classmates, or to predict the answers of peers on a specific questionnaire.[28] Using children at a summer camp, Yarrow and Campbell[29] asked each child to choose one child he felt he knew most about and to "tell all about him as if you were telling a friend back home."

In the analysis or evaluation of the children's responses in all of the above studies, two general approaches were used. One approach was to categorize the type of response the child gave, using a system of levels of difficulty or complexity, and making no attempt to give scores to the children. The second approach was to set up a scoring system of some kind or to establish criteria against which the child's responses could be compared and evaluated. For example, predicted sociometric ratings were compared with actual ratings or answers. In other studies, the correct response was predetermined by the experi-

---

[24] J. E. Bathurst, *op. cit.*; Rosalind F. Dymond, Anne S. Hughes, and Virginia L. Raabe, *op. cit.*

[25] Jui-Ching Hsia, *op. cit.*; C. C. Gibbons and J. P. Porter, *op. cit.*

[26] R. H. Ojemann, *et al.*, "The effects of a 'causal' teacher-training program and certain curricular changes on grade-school children," *J. Exp. Educ.*, XXIV (1955), 95–114.

[27] Esther Kite Harris, "The responsiveness of kindergarten children to the behavior of their fellows," *Monogr. Soc. Res. Child Developm.*, XI (1946), No. 2.

[28] D. P. Ausubel, *op. cit.*; D. P. Ausubel and H. M. Schiff, *op. cit.*; D. P. Ausubel, H. M. Schiff, and E. B. Gasser, *op cit.*; R. V. Miller, *op. cit.*; J. R. Davitz, *op. cit.*

[29] Marian Radke-Yarrow and J. D. Campbell, *op. cit.*

menter, who selected photographs of an actress expressing specific emotions or had the artist draw a specific picture. The largest number of studies, however, used "experts" to establish criteria against which the child's responses were evaluated.

Employing a different approach, Lois Murphy[30] made an observational study of children's expressions of sympathy in actual social situations at the nursery school level, and discovered that the older children responded to a wider range of distress situations and more actively tried to comfort, help, or defend a troubled child than did younger children.

Limitations of Previous Assessment Techniques

Most of the empirical studies that have been carried out in the past have certain limitations. Where the child was required to recall some earlier experiences with specified other persons, he was required to do more than just understand some ongoing interaction. His response depended in part on his ability to recall previous experiences and to abstract or generalize from these. Where a verbal description of a social situation was presented to the child, his ability to comprehend and work abstractly with words and ideas was involved. Where the child was asked to make up a story about a still picture, his own personality characteristics may have been reflected as much as his ability to understand social interaction.

Further, any study that focuses on one aspect of expressive behavior, such as facial expression or tone of voice, at a time has definite limitations. In actual social interaction the child probably does not respond to elements of a situation as separate and isolated items, but rather reacts to the situation in its totality.

Of all the studies, only the one by Murphy has attempted to measure understanding as it is manifested in response to "live" social situations, and this involved only one general kind of situation. None of the other studies measured understanding in response to social situations, either actual or as presented on sound film. Nor have the previous studies reported on the *kinds* of understanding a child has or the nature of the changes that take place with age.

Although in the present study the task required verbal responses, the child was not presented with merely verbal cues. Rather, the child was presented with sound-film episodes of ongoing social interaction.

[30] Lois Murphy, *op. cit.*

2

Subjects and Procedure

In this cross-sectional study, there were twenty children at each of three age levels (six, nine, and twelve).

Since previous studies had found a sex difference in the particular abilities studied or measured,[1] it was decided to limit the study to one sex — girls. In this way a limited number of cases could be used more effectively.

Other studies have also suggested that ability to understand social interaction might be related to intelligence. Therefore it was decided in this study to use only children of average or near-average intelligence (as indicated by scores on intelligence tests administered under the auspices of the school the children attended).

As a control for socioeconomic factors, only children from a middle-class neighborhood were used.

The subjects all attended an elementary school in a middle-class community near New York City. The principal, on request, drew up a list of names of children who would participate in the study and who met these specifications: girls whose IQ, according to the school records, was between 90–115, and whose birthdays fell between specified dates.

[1] E. S. Gollin, "Organizational characteristics of social judgment: A developmental investigation," *J. Pers.*, XXVI (1958), 139–54; W. H. Winch, "Children's perceptions," *Educ. Psychol. Mongr.*, No. 12 (Baltimore: Warwick and York, 1914); D. P. Ausubel, "Socioempathy as a function of sociometric status in an adolescent group," *Human Relat.*, VIII (1955), 75–84; Georgina Strickland Gates, "An experimental study of the growth of social perception," *J. Educ. Psychol.*, XIV (1923), 449–61; Esther Kite Harris, "The responsiveness of kindergarten children to the behavior of their fellows," *Monogr. Soc. Res. Child Develpm.*, XI (1946), No. 2; W. E. Walton, "Empathic responses in children," *Psychol. Monogr.*, XLVIII (1936), 40–67.

Filmed Episodes of Social Interaction for Observation

The procedure used in this study was to present sound-film clips portraying episodes of social interaction. After the showing of each episode, the children were asked to give, in their own words, an account of what had happened. Following this, they were asked a uniform set of questions to elicit their interpretations or explanations of particular happenings within each episode.

Selection of the Filmed Episodes

The decision to present episodes of social interaction by means of sound films was based on several considerations. The films provide a uniform stimulus situation such as could not be insured if a "live" dramatization were repeated again and again. Sound films present concrete situations for the child to observe, and can approximate social reality in the interaction that is presented. To a large degree, the actions that are depicted, combined with the dialogue and other sounds, define what there is for the child to hear and see. Sound films are more realistic and more differentiated than still pictures, and to a much smaller degree require the child to draw on his own "projections" when he is asked to interpret what he sees. Sound films also enable the researcher to retain some of the complexity of lifelike situations, while controlling what is exposed for observation and providing a standardized form of presentation.

In the preliminary work of this study, many movies were examined and discarded. These included movies directed primarily at adults or educational movies contrived to convey a particular message.

During the course of an extensive survey of films that might be used, several criteria were developed to aid in the final selection:

1. The sound film should present a situation that has some similarity to the experience of most children (as judged by the investigator).

2. The sound film should consist primarily of dialogue and overt action to be interpreted, rather than narration that interprets the scene for the viewer.

3. The sound film should be able to hold the interest of child-observers.

4. The sound film should present behavior that could elicit responses at different levels of complexity, ranging from reports of obvious happenings to more sophisticated interpretation.

5. The sound films should portray a variety of feelings, a variety of motivations, a variety of family relationships, and a variety of social situations.

After many films had been tried with children and discarded, it was decided to 'use two dramatic selections from the commercial film *Our Vines Have Tender Grapes,* and permission was obtained for this from Films, Inc. Each contained a sequence of events that constituted a complete, self-contained story, with an introductory scene establishing a "problem," intervening scenes on the same theme, and a scene concluding the action dealing with the theme.

Preliminary Study

A preliminary trial of the films, with ten boys and girls between the ages of six and ten, was carried out to see whether the method was feasible, and to get the children's spontaneous reactions to the selected film excerpts. These preliminary efforts showed that it *was* feasible to use film excerpts as a means of eliciting the sought-for information from school-age children. However, it seemed clear that the filmed excerpts presented for observation in the final study would have to be short in order to hold the child's attention and to make sure that the report on the excerpts would not predominantly serve to measure a child's memory. Even a ten- to fifteen-minute excerpt was too long and had to be subdivided.

During the preliminary trial of the films, an unstructured interview was conducted, using only general questions such as, "What happened in this movie?" The child's response to the general questions was often meager and did not seem to represent all that the child saw and understood, whereas subsequent specific questioning elicited material that the child had not mentioned when he first told about the film strip in his own way.

A second trial of the films was carried out, with girls only and extending the lower age downward to four years. Four four-year olds, four six-year olds, and four eight-year olds were tested. Each film selection was shown in five parts rather than as one continuous whole, and each part was from one-and-a-half to three minutes in length. This procedure had several advantages. It put a minimum of strain on the younger children's ability to concentrate. It meant there was less for the child to keep in mind, and it offered a limited piece of interaction to observe and discuss. It insured that subsequent verbal cues in the movie did not give clues to the answers for the questions asked in the interview. And, it enabled the child to respond at a number of different points, thereby furnishing a larger sample of his responses.

11

It became clear that in order to compare the answers of one child with those of other children in a systematic manner, it would be necessary in the final study to have standardized questions on the movies. To accomplish this, it was necessary to do a content analysis of the sound films.

As noted, the selections from *Our Vines Have Tender Grapes* represented a complete dramatic interlude, one episode leading to the next and reaching a climax in the style of a finished film strip. The two selections are here referred to as Movie A and Movie B. The five parts into which each movie was divided are referred to as episodes.

Synopses of Episodes[2]

Movie A

Episode 1. A girl is practicing skating with a new pair of skates. A visiting boy demands a turn and she tries to put him off. There is an argument, and the boy calls the girl a pig who eats slop and begins shouting, "I want a turn." The girl's mother, looking out of the window of the house, seems exasperated and annoyed as she tells the girl to let the boy have the skates "this minute." The girl says, "All right," but then in an angry voice calls him a tattletale and tries to get him to go home. He threatens to tell. Angrily, she pushes him down and he runs toward the house, calling the girl's mother.

Episode 2. The mother informs the father the girl won't let the boy play with the skates. The father suggests the mother spank the girl. She says it is his job. He replies he can't do it, his hand's too big, and he might hurt her. The mother states she is busy making supper. In an angry tone, the father then asks the girl why she didn't give the boy a turn. She explains that the boy called her a pig who eats slop. The father asks the boy if he said it, and in an innocent tone, the boy says, "No." The girl angrily calls him a liar. In a harsh, brusque tone, the father orders the girl to give the boy the skates. Defiantly, the girl says, "No." The father states that unless she gives the boy the skates she will have to go to bed without supper. The girl takes off her skates and announces she is going to bed without supper. The father, surprised and annoyed, says, "Give me those skates." Having misunderstood, the girl points out that he said if she went to bed without supper, she didn't

---

[2] The synopses of Movies A and B represent not only a literal account of the action and dialogue but also what two judges agreed the writer apparently intended to convey and the actors apparently intended to express. A complete transcript of Movie A and Movie B can be found in the author's Ph.D. dissertation, "Children's Understanding of Social Interaction" (Columbia University, 1965).

have to give the boy a turn. The father says she now doesn't have to give the boy a turn, but has to give him the skates as a present. The girl is crushed as he sends her to her room. The father shows some guilt as well as sadness as she leaves. The boy states, "She sure is selfish," and appears complacent and victorious.

Episode 3. In the living room, the father is looking at a newspaper, but he finds it impossible to concentrate and keeps looking up in the direction of the girl's bedroom. The girl looks down and asks to kiss him good night. He is uncomfortable as he tells her to go back to bed. Again he tries to read the newspaper, but soon gives up and goes into the kitchen. He looks troubled as he tells the mother he is going to take a bath. As he starts to leave, she mentions a circus is going through town in the early morning hours, realizing he will get the idea of taking the girl to see it. The father, seeing this as a way to "make it up" to his daughter, thanks the mother.

Episode 4. As the circus trucks pass, and there is nothing to look at, the girl disappointedly says, "They're only pictures." Suddenly, the girl sees an elephant's head sticking above an open truck and excitedly asks if he is going to come out. The father goes over to the truck-driver and asks. When the driver says, "Nope," the father offers to pay. The driver asks for five dollars. The father counts out every cent he has, which amounts to four dollars, and the driver agree to take the elephant out. The father returns to his daughter and tells her the driver "is always glad to show elephants to little girls." As she watches the elephant perform tricks, the girl shows unrestrained excitement and enthusiasm. Because of her whole-hearted reaction, the truck-driver asks if she would like a ride on the elephant's trunk. The girl is speechless, as well as thrilled, as she gets on the trunk, and scared as she has a ride. The father is a little uneasy but then relaxes and enjoys her happiness.

Episode 5. Riding home in the car, the father says she will be in bed before the sun comes up. The girl asks whether this time she can kiss him good night. In his "Yes" there is love, and relief that all turned out well. The girl says she is sorry about the afternoon, and the father says he knows. She states this has been the nicest summer of her life. He assures her she will have more, and they'll be nicer.

Movie B

Episode 1. The girl and boy are walking along the road, talking about what they are going to be when they grow up. When he states he is going to be a soldier and shoot, she claims she will be a WAC and shoot more than he. He says she won't because she is a girl. She tries to "show him" how she will shoot by throwing a rock at a squirrel. The rock kills the squirrel, which surprises and grieves the girl. Crying, she says she didn't mean to kill it. The boy points out that red squirrels are bad. The girl explains that the squirrel was just eating and wasn't doing anything bad when she threw the rock and that she almost never hits where she aims.

Episode 2. The children run around the side of the house into the yard. The mother tells them to ring the dinner bell and then wash. Both want to pull the bell. The boy reminds her he is "the guest," and she reluctantly gives in. The children run over to a pump and pump water for each other to wash with. As the children wash their hands, the mother reminds the girl to wash her face, too. The girl says she didn't touch anything with her face, but then obeys her mother.

Episode 3. As the father enters the yard, the children run over to greet him. While the father unhooks his horse and puts away his plow, the children climb on the fence. Then in a troubled and uneasy voice the girl asks if red squirrels are bad. The father answers in a matter-of-fact, nonchalant way, until he notices that she is troubled and then asks what the matter is. She tells him. The boy joins in to state the girl picked up a rock and "killed him dead." The father points out that she didn't mean to. But she seems inconsolable as she says it isn't what you mean to do but what you do. The father then tries to cheer her and to take her mind off what has happened by announcing he has a present for her in the barn.

Episode 4. In the barn is a cow and newborn calf. The girl is thrilled and unbelieving as she asks if the calf is really her own. The father obviously enjoys her pleasure. She asks if she can take care of it and he replies if a girl has a calf, she *has* to take care of it. She asks whether the calf might have been born while she was killing the squirrel. The father answers that it probably was. Meantime, the boy is watching the calf and wonders aloud how it is going to get dry if the cow keeps on licking it.

Episode 5. The mother is serving dinner to the other three at the kitchen table. The girl is excited and enthusiastic about her calf. The boy announces that if he had a calf it would be bigger, only "I haven't got a calf." The mother matter-of-factly says the girl doesn't either. The mother tries to say that it is "just pretend" her calf. But the girl denies this. The mother explains that on a farm everything belong to the whole family and not just to one person, and looks to the father for agreement. The father, uneasy and awkward, states that this may have been what he meant to say but that he did tell the girl it was hers. Then reluctantly, he says maybe they should "figure it" the way the mother said. The girl is completely crushed and unhappy. As the mother notices the girl's face, she changes her mind and states it may be a "good thing" for the girl to have something to take care of. The girl looks happy again and the boys wonders aloud if the calf knows who it belongs to.

Interview Questions

A detailed analysis was made of each of the five episodes in Movie A and Movie B as a basis for raising specific questions about significant events in each episode, events setting the stage for the next step in the drama and events presenting distinct actions or interactions that could be described with varying degrees of perceptiveness.

Twenty-eight questions were formulated for Movie A and twenty-four for Movie B. (These interview questions may be found in Appendix A.)

It had become apparent during the preliminary study that some children began to be fatigued when both movies were shown at one sitting. It was therefore decided to show the movies in two sittings — one for each movie. The showing of each movie and the interviewing usually lasted from thirty-five to forty-five minutes.

Procedure

In the main study, with sixty children (twenty children at each of three age levels), each child was individually shown and questioned about the two film selections, on separate occasions a week apart. Half the children were shown Movie A first and half were shown Movie B first.

Before the film was shown, the child was told that "we are interested in finding out what children see when they look at movies. This might help us in the future in making movies for children." An effort was made to give the orientation that the child was a participant in a search for knowledge, that she was *not* taking a test in which there were "right" and "wrong" answers. She was also told that "different children see the same film in different ways" and that she was "the *only* one who could tell me what *she* saw in the movie."

Immediately following each of the five episodes in each film, the sound film was stopped and the child was told, "Pretend I didn't see the movie and tell me what happened," and her account of what happened was recorded verbatim. Following this, standardized questions were asked, as described above, to determine the kinds of interpretations of feelings and thoughts and the kinds of explanations of behavior the child gave when her attention was directed to specific happenings in each episode.

15

3

Children's Own Accounts of What Happened

Two procedures were applied in evaluating and scoring the children's responses. One covered the child's own account in response to the direction, "Pretend I didn't see the movie and tell me what happened" (the unstructured part of the interview). The other covered the responses to the structured part of the interview, consisting of the twenty-eight questions used with Movie A and the twenty-five questions used with Movie B. This chapter will present the evaluation of the children's own accounts of what happened, and the findings that resulted. Chapter IV will present the evaluation of the children's responses to the interview questions, and the findings that resulted.

Treatment of the Children's Own Accounts of What Happened

Categories Used in Evaluation

The categories used in evaluating the children's own accounts of what happened in the movies were designed to reflect as closely as possible the ways in which the children themselves organized and conceptualized their observations. Tentative categories were based on the material that accumulated in the first exploratory trial of the films. These were refined and reformulated on an empirical basis in further exploratory work with the films. From this, and for the final study, three major categories evolved: (1) reporting-describing; (2) explaining; and (3) inferring-interpreting. Each of these categories was further divided into subcategories. (The instructions used by the judges in categorizing the children's statements may be found in Appendix A.)

The "reporting-describing" category contained five subcategories:

1. Reporting or describing the objective details of the *situation* or *action,* such as, "It was summer"; "The girl was skating."
2. Reporting the *verbal communication.* Any repetition or summary of the content of the dialogue, such as, "He said, 'You are a pig.'"
3. Reporting or describing *expressive behavior,* such as, "She was crying."
4. Reporting or describing *obvious feelings.* A tally was made here if the feeling a child mentioned was one that was specifically mentioned in the dialogue of the film, such as, "The girl said she was happy," or was obviously manifested by the expressive behavior or the action, such as, "She is crying, she feels sad." (However, if the child went beyond the dialogue and expressive behavior, the statement was categorized under "inferring-interpreting.")
5. Reporting or describing *obvious intentions.* This covered any report of an intention that was specifically mentioned in the dialogue of the film or that was obviously manifested by the action, such as "The boy said he wanted to skate." (However, if the child went beyond the dialogue and the action, the statement was categorized under "inferring-interpreting.")

The "explaining" category was divided into three subcategories:

1. Explaining in *situational terms.* Any statement that gave an account of the overt action that had occurred, or of the feelings, intentions, thoughts, perceptions, in terms of the objective situation or the overt action or the dialogue, such as, "She was sad because the squirrel was dead"; "He rang the bell because he was the guest."
2. Explaining in *psychological terms.* Any statement that gave an explanation of an observation in terms of an actor's feelings, intentions, or thoughts, such as, "She was sad because she thought her father didn't love her"; "He wanted to take her to the circus because he wanted to make up for what he had done."
3. Explaining in terms of *interpersonal perceptions.* Any statement that gave an explanation of an observation in terms of one actor's perception of another actor's feelings, intentions, or thoughts, such as, "The mother changed her mind because she saw that her daughter was unhappy"; "The man offered her a ride because he saw how thrilled she was."

The "inferring-interpreting" category was divided into four subcategories:

1. Inferring or interpreting *feelings not obviously expressed* (as by crying) *and not specifically labeled.* If the child went beyond the

17

dialogue and expressive behavior and mentioned a feeling that was not obvious, such as, "The girl felt disappointed," or if the child mentioned a combination of mixed feelings, such as, "He felt surprised and angry," the statement was categorized as inferring-interpreting a subtle feeling.

2. Inferring-interpreting *intentions not obviously expressed and not specifically labeled.* If a child went beyond the dialogue and the action and mentioned an intention that was not obvious, such as, "He didn't want her to get the wrong impression," the statement was categorized as inferring-interpreting a subtle intention.

3. Inferring-interpreting *thoughts or expectations.* Any statement that a child made that attributed an unexpressed thought or an expectation to an actor, such as "She expected him to believe her"; "She thought her mother was being mean."

4. Inferring-interpreting *interpersonal perceptions.* Any mention of an actor's observation of another actor's feelings, intentions, or thoughts, such as, "He saw how happy she was"; "The mother saw that the girl was sad."

In connection with each episode of the film, the child's complete response to the instruction, "Pretend I didn't see the movie and tell me what happened," was considered as one unit. This response was read and evaluated in its entirety to determine the presence or absence of *any* statement or statements falling into each of the various subcategories. The child was given a tally of one in a given subcategory in connection with each of the five episodes in each movie whether he had made one or several responses fitting the particular subcategory.

For example, a six-year-old said about Episode 1 of Movie A, "The boy wanted those skates. And the boy said she was a dirty pig. And then the boy told the lady about it. And the girl pushed him down."

The first statement, "The boy wanted those skates," was categorized as reporting the intention that was obvious from the dialogue and from the action. The next statement, "And the boy said she was a dirty pig," was categorized as reporting the verbal communication. The third statement, "And then the boy told the lady about it," was also categorized as reporting the verbal communication. The last statement, "And the girl pushed him down," was categorized as reporting the situation-action. Although four statements were made, two of these fell in the same subcategory, with the result that the child received three separate tallies as follows: one for reporting an obviously expressed intention, one for reporting a verbal communication, and one for reporting a situation-action. All of these tallies fell in subcategories under the general heading of reporting or describing what literally happened or what actually was said.

In talking about the same episode, a nine-year-old said:

The girl was skating around like a tower. And there was a boy there, and he wanted his turn. But she didn't want to give him his turn. So he told her, "If you don't give me my turn, I'll tell Aunt Bruna." And she wouldn't. So he called her a dirty pig that ate slop. Then Aunt Bruna hollered out and said, "What's the matter?" And the boy told her that Selma wouldn't let him take his turn on the roller skates. So the aunt told Selma to give him his turn. Then she got mad and said, "I'll give you your turn, but you better not tell." And he started to tell. So she pushed him to the ground. And he got up and ran to tell Aunt Bruna.

This was categorized as follows:

The girl was skating around like a tower.	Report of situation-action
And there was a boy there,	Report of situation-action
and he wanted his turn.	Report of obvious intention
But she didn't want to give him his turn.	Report of obvious intention
So he	Explanation in terms of an intention
told her, "If you don't give me my turn, I'll tell Aunt Bruna."	Report of verbal communication
And she wouldn't.	Report of situation-action
So he	Explanation in terms of situation-action
called her a dirty pig that ate slop.	Report of verbal communication
Then Aunt Bruna hollered out and said, "What's the matter?"	Report of verbal communication
And the boy told her that Selma wouldn't let him take his turn on the roller skates.	Report of verbal communication
So the aunt	Explanation in terms of what another said
told Selma to give him his turn.	Report of verbal communication
Then she got mad	Report of obvious feeling

19

and said, "I'll give you your turn, but you better not tell."	Report of verbal communication
And he started to tell.	Report of situation-action
So she	Explanation in terms of situation-action
pushed him to the ground.	Report of situation-action
And he got up	Report of situation-action
and ran to tell Aunt Bruna.	Report of situation-action

This child was given a tally of one for one or more statements in each of the following categories: reporting the situation-action, reporting verbal communication, reporting an obviously expressed feeling, reporting an obvious intention, explaining an action in terms of the situation-action or in terms of what another said, and explaining an action in terms of an intention.

Agreement in Classifying the Statements

Two procedures were used to assess the suitability and effectiveness of the scheme used to analyze the data in this part of the study. One consisted of comparing the categorizations made by two independent workers. The other consisted of comparing the categorizations made by one worker on two different occasions a week apart.

In measuring interjudge agreement, two judges independently categorized all of the spontaneous statements of the first seven children of each of the three age groups. The percent agreement of these judges ranged between 100 percent for almost all of the reporting-describing categories and 80 percent for the category of inferring-interpreting intentions for the six-year-olds (which is also the category with the smallest number of statements). Taking all of the statements together, the percent agreement between judges for each of the three age-groups was 99.[2]

In measuring intrajudge agreement, the same judge categorized all of the statements of all of the children on two different occasions a week apart. Again the percent agreement ranged between 100 percent for the majority of the reporting-describing categories and 80 percent for the category of inferring-interpreting intentions for the six-year-olds (which again was the category with the smallest number of state-

[2] See Appendix B, Table 7, showing agreement between judges.

ments). Again, taking all of the statements together, the percent agreement on two different occasions for each of the three age groups was 99.[3]

As might be expected, the percent agreement was highest for the reporting-describing categories (which could easily be checked against the typed transcript of the movies) and was lowest for the inferring-interpreting categories, which are also little-used categories.

Consistency of the Types of Response the Children Gave to the Two Movies

The categorized responses given by the children when telling, in their own words, what happened in Movie A were compared with the responses they gave to Movie B. Table 1 shows the number of children in each age group who used statements classified within each category in talking about both movies, in talking about one movie, and who never used statements within the category.

As can be seen, there was much more consistency than inconsistency. Some children were "consistent" in using statements of a given category in talking about *both* movies. Other children were "consistent" in *never* using statements of a given category in talking about either movie. Where there is inconsistency, it shows a developmental trend, statements classified within the given category being used not at all or very little by the six-year-olds and in talking about both movies by a few nine-year-olds, and then being used more consistently in talking about both movies by the twelve-year-olds.

The highest consistency appears for all three age groups to be in the use of statements classified in the category of reporting-describing the situation-action and in the category of reporting verbal communication, both of these kinds of statements being used by all children in all age groups. The six-year-olds also showed perfect consistency in *not* using statements classified in the category of inferring-interpreting feelings, in *not* using statements classified in the category of inferring-interpreting interpersonal perceptions, and in *not* using statements classified in the category of explaining in terms of interpersonal perceptions, in talking about either movie.

Consistency in Length of Response

The consistency of a child's performance was assessed also by noting the number of statements made by each child in giving her own account of each of the two movies. The rank order of the number of

---

[3] See Appendix B, Table 8, showing agreement between two categorizations, one week apart, by one judge.

TABLE 1

Consistency of the Children in Using Various Types of Statements in Telling What Happened in the Movies

(N at each age is 20)

Categories of statements	Six-year-olds			Nine-year-olds			Twelve-year-olds		
	Number who used category in telling about both movies	Number who used category in telling about one movie	Number who never used category	Number who used category in telling about both movies	Number who used category in telling about one movie	Number who never used category	Number who used category in telling about both movies	Number who used category in telling about one movie	Number who never used category
Reporting and describing									
Situation-action	20	0	0	20	0	0	20	0	0
Verbal communication	20	0	0	20	0	0	20	0	0
Expressive behavior	10	6	4	8	9	3	11	6	3
Obvious feelings	15	4	1	15	4	1	19	1	0
Obvious intentions	5	8	7	18	2	0	19	1	0
Interpreting-inferring									
Feelings	0	0	20	6	7	7	10	8	2
Thoughts-expectations	1	1	18	7	6	7	9	6	5
Intentions-motives	1	1	18	3	3	14	5	5	10
Interpersonal perceptions	0	0	20	0	4	16	3	4	13
Explaining									
In situational terms	9	1	10	14	5	1	16	3	1
In psychological terms	1	2	17	5	7	8	10	4	6
In terms of interpersonal perceptions	0	0	20	0	6	14	2	4	14

statements made in responses to one movie was compared with the rank order for the other movie. The correlations were moderate, but again showed a developmental trend. The correlation was .50 at the six-year level, .60 at the nine-year level, and .73 at the twelve-year level.

Analysis of Responses When the Children Gave Their Own Accounts

Table 2 shows the number of children in each age group who made one or more statements that were classified in each of the categories used in analyzing the children's accounts of what happened in the movies. The maximum number possible for each entry is 20, corresponding to the number of children in each group. (An explanation of the statistical significance of the findings may be found in Appendix A-3).

No differences appeared between the three age groups in the number of children who used statements classified in most of the subcategories of simply reporting or describing. All children at all three ages used statements in the category that reported-described the situation in which the interaction occurred or reported-described the physical movements of the actors; all children at all three ages used statements in the category that includes a more or less verbatim repetition of what the actors actually said; practically all children at all three ages used statements in the category that reported-described expressive behavior such as crying and laughing; and practically all children at all three ages used statements in the category that reported-described feelings an adult would consider obvious, such as feeling happy or feeling sad. There was a difference, however, between the six-year-olds and the two older groups in connection with reports of intentions. Only 13 of the six-year-olds reported intentions that from an adult's viewpoint were quite obvious, while all of the nine-year-olds and all of the twelve-year-olds reported such intentions. While the difference is not statistically significant, the fact that there is a difference between the six-year-olds and the two older groups, and the fact that there is not a difference between the nine-year-olds and the twelve-year-olds, suggests a transitional period between six and nine years.

A developmental trend also appeared in the use of statements classified within the category that includes explanations of several kinds. The difference between the six-year-olds and the two older age groups is statistically significant in the use of statements that attempted to account for an action in terms of the just preceding or the presently ongoing situation or the setting of the action. The number of children increased with age from 10 six-year-olds to 19 nine-year-olds and 19 twelve-year-olds who gave explanations of this kind. There was not a

23

statistically significant difference in the use of statements classified in the other subcategories of explaining, but again there is a suggestion of a developmental trend. Only 3 six-year-olds attempted to account for the ongoing action in terms of an actor's own feelings, thoughts or intentions, while 12 nine-year-olds and 14 twelve-year-olds gave explanations in these terms. None of the six-year-olds attempted to account for the ongoing action in terms of one actor's perception of another actor's feeling, thoughts, or intentions, while 6 nine-year-olds and 6 twelve-year-olds offered explanations in these terms. As with the use of statements classified as "reporting-describing," there were impressive differences between the six-year-olds and the two older groups. However, the number of nine-year-olds and the number of twelve-year-olds who used statements classified as attempting to explain the action were quite similar.

TABLE 2

Number of Children at Each Age Level Who, in Their Accounts of What Happened in the Movies, Used Statements Classified in the Various Categories

(N at each age is 20)

Categories of statements	Number of six-year-olds	Number of nine-year-olds	Number of twelve-year-olds
Reporting and describing			
Situation-action	20	20	20
Verbal communication	20	20	20
Expressive behavior	16	17	17
Obvious feelings	19	19	20
Obvious intentions	13	20	20
Explaining			
In situational terms	10	19	19
In psychological terms	3	12	14
In terms of interpersonal perceptions	0	6	6
Interpreting-inferring			
Feelings	0	13	18
Thoughts-expectations	2	13	15
Intentions-motives	2	6	10
Interpersonal perceptions	0	4	7

Differences between the six-year-olds and the other two age groups become more apparent in the use of statements that were classified within the subcategories of interpreting-inferring. The differences are statistically significant in the use of statements classified within the subcategory of "interpreting-inferring feelings" and within the subcategory of "interpreting-inferring thoughts and expectations." In fact, none of the six-year-olds mentioned feelings that were not obviously expressed or not specifically labeled, while 13 of the nine-year-olds and 18 of the twelve-year-olds commented on these more subtle feelings. Two of the six-year-olds mentioned thoughts of an actor, but this contrasts with 13 nine-year-olds and 15 twelve-year-olds who inferred such thoughts.

While the differences are not statistically significant between the three age groups in the use of statements classified as "interpreting-inferring intentions" and statements classified as "interpreting-inferring interpersonal perceptions," it is interesting that there is a progression in the use of both kinds of statements. Two of the six-year-olds mentioned intentions or motives of an actor that were not obviously expressed or specifically labeled in the interaction. This can be compared with 6 nine-year-olds and 10 twelve-year-olds who inferred such intentions or motives. None of the six-year-olds inferred one actor's perception of another actor's feelings, thoughts, or intentions, and this can be compared with 4 nine-year-olds and 7 twelve-year-olds who inferred such perceptions.

It is of interest to note that wherever there are statistically significant differences between the six-year-olds and the twelve-year-olds, there are also statistically significant differences between the six-year-olds and the nine-year-olds. There are no statistically significant differences between the nine-year-olds and the twelve-year-olds, but there does appear some progression in several of the subcategories of "explaining" and of "interpreting-inferring."

Patterns of Response

The statements made by the children and classified in the various categories were also analyzed to determine the patterns of categories into which the statements fell. The several patterns are presented on the following page, in Table 3.

Again it can be noted that there is a developmental trend. Many of the six-year-olds fit into a pattern of using reporting statements but making *no* use of any interpreting-inferring statements or any explaining statements. About the same number of six-year-olds fit into the pattern of using reporting statements *and* explaining statements, but *no* interpreting-inferring statements. Only three fit the pattern of using reporting, explaining, *and* interpreting-inferring statements.

These results seem to indicate that the use of descriptive terms and reporting of the content of the dialogue (often in verbatim terms) develops before the use of explanatory statements or the use of statements involving inference and interpretation, and the use of explanatory statements before the use of statements of inference or intepretation.

The development moving in the direction from reporting to explaining to interpreting-inferring also seems to appear with the two age groups. Only one nine-year-old and none of the twelve-year-olds showed the pattern of using reporting kinds of statements but *no* interpreting-inferring and *no* explaining statements. Four nine-year-olds but none of the twelve-year-olds showed the pattern of using reporting statements *and* explaining statements but *no* interpreting-inferring statements. All of the rest, 15 nine-year-olds, showed the pattern of using reporting statements, explaining statements, *and* interpreting-inferring statements; and *all* 20 of the twelve-year-olds showed one or the other of the two most complex patterns — using reporting statements, explanatory statements, and/or interpreting-inferring statements.

TABLE 3

Number of Children at Each Age Level Who, in Their Accounts of What Happened in the Movies, Showed Various Patterns
of Categories of Statements
(N at each age is 20)

Pattern of categories	Number of six-year-olds	Number of nine-year-olds	Number of twelve-year-olds
Reporting statements, but *no* explaining statements and *no* interpreting-inferring statements	8	1	0
Reporting statements *and* explaining statements, but *no* interpreting inferring statements	9	4	0
Reporting statements *and* interpreting-inferring statements, but *no* explaining statements	0	0	1
Reporting statements, explaining statements, *and* interpreting-inferring statements	3	15	19

A further analysis was made of just the responses of children whose statements were classified within the category of "explaining," and here, too, a developmental trend appeared, as can be seen in Table 4. Most of the six-year-olds who used statements that explained, phrased their explanations in situational terms and did not use any statements that explained in psychological terms or any statements that explained in terms of interpersonal perceptions. For example, a six-year-old would say, "She was crying because the squirrel was dead," whereas a twelve-year-old would say, "She started crying because she felt sorry for what she did" [killing the squirrel].

A few (three) of the six-year-olds fitted the pattern of using statements that explained in situational terms and/or statements that explained in psychological terms but not using any statements that explained in terms of interpersonal perceptions. No six-year-old used a statement that explained in terms of interpersonal perceptions. For example, a twelve-year-old said, "He [the father] looked at the girl and he saw she was so excited . . . and he was willing to pay for the elephant to come out," whereas six-year-olds did not mention the observation by one actor of another actor's psychological state.

TABLE 4

Number of Children at Each Age Level Who, in Their Accounts of What Happened in the Movies, Showed Various Patterns of Statements within the Subcategories of the Explaining Category

(N at each age is 20)

Patterns of statements	Number of six-year-olds	Number of nine-year-olds	Number of twelve-year-olds
Statements that explain in situational terms, but *no* statements that explain in psychological terms and *no* statements that explain in terms of interpersonal perceptions	9	7	4
Statements that explain in situational terms and/or statements that explain in psychological terms, but *no* statements that explain in terms of interpersonal perceptions	3	6	9
Statements that explain in situational terms and/or statements that explain in psychological terms and/or statements that explain in terms of interpersonal perceptions	0	6	6

The present data suggests that the use of explanations in situational terms occurs before the use of explanations in psychological terms and that the use of explanations in psychological terms occurs before the use of explanations in terms of interpersonal perceptions.

This development, moving from situational kinds of explanations to psychological kinds of explanations to explanations in terms of interpersonal perceptions also seems to appear with the two older age groups. Twice as many nine-year-olds as six-year-olds (6 as compared with 3) fitted into the pattern of using statements that explained in situational terms and/or statements that explained in psychological terms but no statements that explained in terms of interpersonal perceptions, while the largest grouping of twelve-year-olds fitted into this pattern. Six of the nine-year-olds and 6 of the twelve-year-olds showed the pattern of using statements that explained in situational terms and/or statements that explained in psychological terms and/or statements that explained in terms of interpersonal perceptions. For example, one twelve-year-old said, "The father was also happy *because* he did something that he knew she liked. . . . And then he told her she would have better summers yet after that *because* he saw how excited she was about seeing the circus."

A similar kind of analysis was made of just the responses of children whose statements were categorized within the "inferring-interpreting" category. Here, too, a developmental trend appeared, as shown in Table 5. All of the six-year-olds whose statements were classified within this category made statements that inferred-interpreted thoughts and/or intentions, but *no* statements that inferred-interpreted feelings or inferred-interpreted interpersonal perceptions. While two of the nine-year-olds fitted into this same pattern, eleven nine-year-olds fitted into the pattern of using statements that inferred thoughts and/or intentions and/or statements that inferred feelings but no statements that inferred interpersonal perceptions. Two nine-year-olds went beyond this and fitted into the pattern of using statements that inferred thoughts and/or intentions and/or statements that inferred feelings and statements that inferred interpersonal perceptions.

TABLE 5

Number of Children at Each Age Level, Who in Their Account of What Happened in the Movies, Showed Various Patterns of Statements within the Subcategories of the Inferring-Interpreting Category
(N at each age is 20)

Pattern of statements	Number of six-year-olds	Number of nine-year-olds	Number of twelve-year-olds
Statements that infer thoughts and/or intentions but *no* statements that infer feelings or interpersonal perceptions	3	2	2
Statements that infer thoughts and/or intentions and/or statements that infer feelings, but *no* statements that infer interpersonal perceptions	0	11	11
Statements that infer thoughts and/or intentions and/or statements that infer feelings and statements that infer interpersonal perceptions	0	2	7

An examination of these two age groups suggests that the use of statements inferring thoughts and/or intentions precedes the use of statements that infer feelings or statements that infer interpersonal perceptions, and that the use of statements that infer feelings precedes the use of statements that infer interpersonal perceptions. The twelve-year-olds seem to uphold this trend, the largest proportion of them fitting into the pattern of using statements that infer thoughts and/or intentions and/or statements that infer feelings but no statements that infer interpersonal perceptions, and considerably more twelve-year-olds than nine-year-olds fitting into the pattern of using statements that infer thoughts and/or intentions and/or statements that infer feelings and statements that infer interpersonal perceptions.

Number of Statements as Related to Categories Used

A difference was noticeable between the number of statements made by the six-year-olds and the number made by the nine- and twelve-year-olds. The six-year-olds as a group made a total of 1,696 statements in giving their own accounts of what happened in the two movies, as compared with a total of 3,250 statements at the nine-year level and 3,192 statements at the twelve-year level. The median number of statements made by the six-year-olds was 48 in response to Movie A and 38 in response to Movie B, by the nine-year-olds, 99 in response to movie A and 64 in response to Movie B, and by the twelve-year-olds, 79 in response to Movie A and 73 in response to Movie B. Even though the total number of statements for the group of nine-year-olds was larger than the total number of statements for the group of twelve-year-olds, and even though the median number of statements for the group of nine-year-olds in response to Movie A was higher than the median number for the group of twelve-year-olds in response to the same movie, it is interesting that a significantly greater number of twelve-year-olds made statements that were classified within the interpreting-inferring categories.

The length of an individual child's response did not seem to be related to a significant degree to the extent to which his statements covered a variety of categories. Sometimes a six-year-old would give a lengthier response than a nine-year-old, yet confine himself to a narrower range of categories. Sometimes six-year-olds would describe very minute details. For example, six-year-olds mentioned, "He wiped his face"; "He cut his food"; "She drank the milk"; "The mother had a bowl" — none of which was mentioned by the nine-year-olds or the twelve-year-olds. This indicated a memory for details, but while reciting such details about the situation or repeating verbatim dialogue they did not make any statements inferring feelings or thoughts. In many instances nine-year-olds and twelve-year-olds gave shorter narratives of what had happened in an episode but offered statements in a wider range of categories.

For example, a six-year-old commented about Episode 5 of Movie B as follows:

> They went in to eat. And they started to eat. And the little girl said, "It's fun to have a calf for your very own." Then the mother said, "It isn't just yours. It's all of ours." Then the girl felt very bad. The girl started to eat. Then the boy said, "If I had a calf, it would be bigger and I would feed it much better." Then the father started to eat his meat. Then Arnold started to take a whole bunch of it. And the mother said, "That's too big for you." And he said, "How come he eats such big bites?" And the lady said, "Because he has a bigger mouth than you."

This account contains 13 statements. All but one statement simply describe the objective situation or overt actions or communications. The one statement that departs from such description ("Then the girl felt very bad") refers to a feeling that was obviously expressed. There is no attempt to infer other feelings, intentions, or interpersonal perceptions, or to give any explanations for what was said.

In talking about the same episode, a twelve-year-old commented as follows:

> Well, they are eating dinner. And the girl asks her father if she can feed the calf. The mother looks puzzled because she hadn't known what it was about. And the boy, out of jealousy, wishes he had one. And the mother tries to show that everything they own is hers and the family's. But the girl wants it to be her own. She wants to have something of her own to take care of. And she is very unhappy when her father says maybe her mother is right. Then they see how sad she looks. And the mother says maybe it is good for her to have something to take care of. And the father agrees. And the girl is very happy about it.

This account contains 18 statements. It includes statements reporting the situation-action, reporting the verbal communication, and reporting obvious feelings, as did the six-year-old's account. But, in addition, it includes statements categorized as reporting obvious intentions; inferring feelings not obviously expressed and intentions that are not openly expressed by word or action; inferring interpersonal perceptions; explaining in terms of the situation-action; and explaining in terms of feelings, thoughts, and intentions.

Another comparison that illustrates the differences between the younger and older children is taken from Episode 3 of Movie B. A six-year-old gave this account:

> The father said, "Come on." So they went with the father. The boy went on the fence first. Then after the boy went on the fence, the girl went on. The girl didn't get on the same way the boy did. So the father lifted the girl down. And so the boy got down the way he got up on the fence. They walked with the father again. The father said, "There is something for you." "What is it?" said the boy. "It is something that just came here today." So the boy put his head under the fence.

Again all of the statements are within the reporting-describing category; in fact this time the statements concentrate on just the situation-action and the verbal communication.

A twelve-year-old gave this account of the same episode:

> The father came in from the field and she told him what they were having for dinner. And then as he was passing, they both got on the fence. And then as he was coming back, she asked if red squirrels were bad, and he said he didn't know. She was trying to get him to say they were. And she said, "Don't they eat your crops?" And he said, "They do eat," but he doesn't mind their eating a little crop. And she looked sad. And he asked her what was the matter. And she said she had killed a red squirrel. And her father said, "You can't help that. You didn't do it on purpose." And she said, "It isn't what you didn't mean to do. It is what you have done." Then he tried to get her so she wasn't upset, so he said he had something in the barn for her and it was something new. And they started walking toward the barn.

Though this account is somewhat lengthier than that of the six-year-old, the bigger contrast is in the content. The twelve-year-old gives a depth and meaning to getting on the fence and getting off and going to the barn that is lacking completely from the account of the six-year-old.

As another example, the following is a comparison of the accounts of a six-year-old and a twelve-year-old in talking about Episode 3 of Movie A. First, the six-year-old's statement:

> At the beginning her daddy was sitting in the chair in the living room looking at the paper, and the little girl got out of her bed and said, "Pa, will you kiss me goodnight?" And the daddy said, "Go to bed," and the little girl went to bed crying. And he tore up the paper and he threw it down on the floor. Then he went into the kitchen and was getting ready to go out to the barn. And the lady said, "Where are you going?" And he said, "Out to the barn." And the lady said, "At this time of the night?" And the man said, "Yes."

Of these 15 statements, all would be included within the reporting-describing category, though this time there is mention of expressive behavior (crying) and mention of an intention (getting ready to go to the barn).

In talking about this same episode a twelve-year-old said:

> The father was reading the newspaper, but he was thinking about something else. He couldn't really read it. And the little girl was looking down and asked her father if he didn't want to kiss her good night. The father wanted to say good night, but then he thought she did something bad, so he said, "No. Go back to bed." And the girl was crying and did go back to bed. And the father tried to read the newspaper again, but he couldn't read it, so he threw it away. He wanted to go up to her and say it wasn't so bad. But he decided he better not. So he went to the kitchen and said to his wife he was going out. And the mother said, "I think you just want to be by yourself." And he said, "Yes." And the mother said, "There is a circus coming to town tonight." I think he is going to go to the circus with the girl now.

This contains a few more statements than the account of the six-year-old, but the striking difference is in the quality of the statements used. In addition to reporting-describing kinds of statements, this child inferred the father's thoughts, conflicts, and intentions and explained the action in psychological terms.

4

The Children's Responses to Structured Interview Questions

Immediately after seeing each episode of the sound film interaction and giving her own spontaneous account of what happened, each child was asked several questions focused on eliciting interpretations of feelings and thoughts and on soliciting explanations for the action that occurred. The responses of the children to the specific interview questions were scored on a three-point scale — 0, 1, and 2. This chapter will present, first, the system used for scoring the responses, and then the findings on the basis of this scoring.

Treatment of the Children's Responses to Structured Interview Questions

The Scoring System for the Children's Responses

To evaluate the child's responses to the specific questions in the interview, adult judges, after observing the film and analyzing the typed transcript, developed a system of scoring each question, ranging from 0 to 2.[1]

Questions asking the child how an actor was feeling. A child was given a score of "0" for a response if, when she was asked how an actor was feeling at a specified moment during the interaction, she answered, "I don't know." A response was also scored "0" if the child named a feeling that represented an interpretation that did not agree with the consensus of adult perceptions. For example, in Episode 1 of Movie A,

[1] For the specific scoring of responses to each interview question for Movie A and Movie B, see the author's Ph.D. dissertation, "Children's Understanding of Social Interaction."

when the mother looked out the window and told the girl to let the boy use the skates, it was obvious to adult judges that the mother was annoyed and irritated. If the child said the mother felt sad or happy, the response was scored "0." Also, the response was scored "0" if there was no mention of feeling, but rather the reporting of an overt action. For example, in Episode 1 of Movie B, it was obvious to adult judges that after the girl threw a rock and accidentally killed a squirrel she felt sad and regretful. A child who answered the question, "How do you think the girl felt after she threw the rock?" and who responded, "She liked squirrels," was given "0" for this response.

A child's response was given a score of "1" if, when asked how an actor was feeling at a specific instant, the child named an overt expressive behavior or if she named an obvious, uncomplicated feeling that had been indicated by the verbal communication or expressive behavior or the overt action, and that agreed with the consensus of adult perceptions. For example, in response to the above question, "How do you think the girl felt after she threw the rock?" a child who responded, "She started to cry," was given a score of "1" for that response, as were also children who said the girl was sad, sorry, feeling bad, or feeling terrible. For Episode 4 of Movie B, in response to the question, "How do you think the girl felt when she first saw the calf?" a child was given a score of "1" for the response, "She said she was happy," as well as for the statements that she felt happy, excited, surprised, nice, good.

A child's response was given a score of "2" if, when asked how an actor was feeling at a specific point in the sound film, the child imputed a feeling or thought to the actor that could be inferred from the action, but that was not explicitly expressed or named, a feeling that was not explicit in either the action or the dialogue. For example, when the question was asked, "How do you think the boy felt while he was looking at the calf?" a response was scored "2" if the child said, "He felt jealous because the father had given it to the girl," or if the child said, "He resented her getting it."

A score of "2" was also given if in her response a child named a combination of two or more simple feelings, which might or might not be compatible but which were plausible and probable under the circumstances. As for instance, when the question was asked, after Episode 2 of Movie A, "How do you think the girl felt after the father gave her skates to the boy?" a score of "2" was given if the child answered, "She felt sorry and mad," or "She felt mad and sad." A score of "2" was given also if the child named a complex combination of feelings and/or thoughts. For example, in answering the question, "How do you think the father felt after he gave the skates to the boy and after the girl went into the house?" a child's response was scored "2" if she said,

"He felt he had done wrong but he couldn't take the skates back," or "He was sorry for the girl but he thought he had to go through with it." Or, in Episode 3 of Movie A, when the question was asked, "How do you think the father felt when the girl asked to kiss him good night?" a child's response was scored "2" if she said, "He wanted to but thought he had to go through with the discipline."

Questions that asked, "Why?" and required some kind of explanation. A child was given a score of "0" for a response if when she was asked why a specific action occurred, she answered, "I don't know" or, "Just because," or if she just repeated the question in statement form. The child's response was also scored "0" if the explanation given did not agree with what the film actually portrayed, as judged objectively by adult judges. In some cases the explanation was of a type that was completely extraneous to the episode shown and could have been given without seeing the movie. For example, in Episode 3 of Movie A, when the father was feeling upset and wanted to be alone, when the question was asked, "Why do you think the father said he was going to take a bath?" some children answered, "He was dirty," or, "He wanted to get warmed up," and these responses were scored "0." An explanation that indicated a misperception of the sequence of events, such as naming an antecedent action as caused by a subsequent action, was also scored "0." For example, in Episode 3 of Movie B, when the girl was looking upset and trying to find a way to tell her father about the squirrel, the father noticed this and asked, "What's the matter?" which then enabled the girl to tell him about having thrown the rock. However, some children when asked, "Why do you think the father asked, 'What's the matter?' after he said he didn't mind the squirrels getting a meal?" answered, "Because she killed the squirrel," and this response was scored "0."

A child was given a score of "1" for a response if, when she was asked why a specific action occurred, she gave an explanation in terms of the factual situation, not inferring any feelings, motives, or thoughts. For example, in Episode 1 of Movie B, when the question was asked, "Why do you think the girl cried after the rock hit the squirrel?" some children said, "Because the squirrel is dead," but made no mention that the girl felt sad or guilty about having killed it. Also, an explanation in terms of the just-preceding action of the film was given a score of "1" as, for instance, when the question was asked about Episode 1 of Movie A, "Why do you think the girl pushed the boy down?" and a child answered, "Because he was going to tell [on her]."

Responses were also scored "1" if they offered an explanation in terms of identifying a simple, obvious feeling, as indicated by the verbal communication or expressive behavior, or if they offered an explanation in terms of mentioning a simple, obvious desire for something by one of the actors, as indicated by the dialogue or action. For Episode 1 of Movie A, the question was asked, "Why do you think the boy called the girl a pig?" If the child said, "Because he wanted a turn on the skates," this was scored "1" since the boy had repeatedly asked for a turn.

A child was given a score of "2" for a response if, when she was asked why a specific action occurred, she gave an explanation in terms of inferring an actor's feeling when such a feeling was not explicitly expressed or named. For example, when the question was asked, "Why do you think the girl cried after the rock hit the squirrel?" a score of "2" was given if the child answered, "Because she felt she did bad in killing the squirrel" or "Because she was sorry she killed him." A score of "2" was given also if the explanation was in terms of attributing a motive or intention that was not explicitly expressed or named. For example, for Episode 2 of Movie A, the question was asked, "Why do you think the mother said she was busy making supper?" The answer, "Because she wanted the father to punish the girl" (an excuse for shifting responsibility), was scored "2."

Explanations in terms of an interpretation of one actor's perception of the situation or perception of a co-actor's feelings, desires, or expectations was also scored "2." For example, for Episode 5 of Movie B, the question was asked, "Why do you suppose the mother changed her mind about [letting the girl keep] the calf?" A child's response was scored "2" if she said, "Because she saw how disappointed the girl was."

On Movie A, 28 questions were asked. Since each question could be scored 0, 1, or 2, there was a possible range of total scores between 0 and 56. On Movie B, 25 questions were asked, so that the possible range was between 0 and 50. Using these scores, the three age-groups were compared with respect to the mean score for each age group, as well as the range of scores for the different groups.

Agreement between Judges in Scoring Responses to Interview Questions

To assess the workability of the analysis of the data, the agreement between judges in scoring was determined, as well as the intrajudge agreement at two different times. As a first step in measuring the interjudge agreement, two judges independently scored 80 items chosen at random, regardless of the question or the age level, for Movie A, scoring these 0, 1, or 2. There was agreement on 75 of the 80 items, or 94 percent. On the five items where there was disagreement, the disagreement was a one-step difference. For example, one judge might mark an item "1" and the other judge mark it "2."

Following this, the two judges independently scored two items chosen at random from the protocols of each of the 20 children at each age level for Movie A and two items chosen at random from the protocols of each of the 20 children at each age level for Movie B.[2] There was perfect agreement on the items scored "0." For the most part, this was because these consisted of "I don't know" answers, which can only be scored in one way. The lowest agreement, 75 percent, occurred in scoring "2" the responses of the six-year-olds. In large part this was due to the fact that there were so few of the answers in this category. Taken as a whole, the interjudge agreement for Movie A was 108 items out of a possible 120, or 90 percent. The interjudge agreement for Movie B, as a whole, was 112 items out of a possible 120, or 93 percent.

In measuring intrajudge agreement, the same judge categorized the answers to all the questions for both movies on two different occasions a week apart. The results are shown in Table 10 in Appendix B. Again, the highest agreement was in scoring "0" and the lowest agreement, 85 percent for Movie A and 81 percent for Movie B, was in scoring "2" for the six-year-olds, which was also the category with the least number of items. The intrajudge agreement for Movie A as a whole was 95 percent for the six-year-olds and the nine-year-olds and 96 percent for the twelve-year-olds. The intrajudge agreement for Movie B as a whole was 95 percent for the six-year-olds, 96 percent for the nine-year-olds, and 97 percent for the twelve-year-olds.

Consistency of the Children in Scores on the Two Movies

To assess the consistency of the children's performance, the children's total scores on Movie A were compared with their scores on Movie B. Correlations were .64 at the six-year level, .67 at the nine-year level, and .82 at the twelve-year level. Again the correlations showed an increase with age, the twelve-year-olds showing the highest degree of consistency in their responses to one movie as compared with the other.

Comparisons of Responses to Structured Interview Questions

A comparison between the mean scores at the three age levels in responses to the structured interview questions is shown in Table 6. As was true with the children's own accounts of what happened, the most marked difference from one age level to the next occurred in the performance of the nine-year-olds as compared with the six-year-olds.

[2] For the results, see Table 9 in Appendix B.

However, there still is a fairly substantial difference between the scores at nine and at twelve.

As shown in Table 6, with a total possible score of 56 on Movie A, the mean score for the six-year-olds was 20.9, that for the nine-year-olds was 33.5, and that for the twelve-year-olds was 40.5. Somewhat similar findings appeared in the scores for the structured interview questions on Movie B. The total possible score for this movie was 50. The mean score of the six-year-olds was 15.6, that of the nine-year-olds was 27.5, and that of the twelve-year-olds was 33.2. Combining the scores for both movies gave mean scores of 36.5, 61.0, and 73.7 respectively for the six-year-olds, nine-year-olds, and twelve-year-olds.

The six-year-olds gave answers that were mostly scored "0" and "1," the nine-year-olds' answers were scored mostly "1," and the twelve-year-olds' answers were scored mostly "1" and "2." In response to Movie A, the six-year-olds gave 191 answers that were scored "0," 323 answers that were scored "1," and only 45 that were scored "2." In response to this same movie, the nine-year-olds were scored "0" on only 73 answers, and received a score of "1" on 306 answers and a score of "2" on 181 answers. The twelve-year-olds were scored "0" on only 41 answers, "1" on 230 answers, and "2" on 289 answers.

With Movie B, the six-year-olds were scored "0" on 223 answers and "1" on 241 answers, while they received a score of "2" on only 36 answers. In contrast, the nine-year-olds received a score of "0" on 89 answers, a score of "1" on 272 answers, and a score of "2" on 139 answers. And again, the twelve-year-olds had fewer answers that were scored "0" (58), and received a score of "1" on 220 answers and a score of "2" on 222 answers.

TABLE 6

Scores of the Various Age-Groups in Responding to the Interview
Questions Regarding Feelings, Intentions, and Sequences
of Behavior in the Movies

	Six-year-olds		Nine-year-olds		Twelve-year-olds	
	Mean score	Standard deviation	Mean score	Standard deviation	Mean score	Standard deviation
Movie A*	20.9	5.2	33.5	6.9	40.5	5.5
Movie B**	15.6	5.9	27.5	5.9	33.2	5.8
Both movies	36.5	10.2	61.0	12.2	73.7	10.7

* The total possible score for 28 questions is 56.
** The total possible score for 25 questions is 50.

Responses to Questions about Feelings

In answering questions about feelings, at age six the children often said they did not know the answer or answered in terms of a feeling that did not agree with the consensus of adult perceptions. Oftentimes, in reporting feelings, a six-year-old would persist in using the same word over and over in response to different questions — for example, he felt good, she felt not good; or she felt sad, he felt not sad; or he felt fine, she felt not fine.

At age nine most of the answers reported obvious, uncomplicated feelings that were mentioned in the dialogue or were clearly presented in the expressive behavior or action. However, there were some answers that mentioned complex or subtle feelings.

At age twelve the children answered in terms of complex combinations of feelings, or inferred feelings that went beyond the dialogue or action, or answered in terms of naming a feeling and then elaborating in terms of the actors' thoughts, intentions, anticipations, or expectations.

Responses to Questions Requiring Explanations of Behavior

In answering questions that called for an explanation of behavior, the six-year-olds often said they did not know or gave answers that were not appropriate to the action of the film, or even explained an antecedent action by something that happened subsequently. In addition, they gave many explanations in terms of the existing situation or the just-preceding action.

The nine-year-olds gave explanations primarily in terms of the existing situation or the just-preceding action, though some gave explanations in psychological terms, such as imputing motives, thoughts, or anticipations to an actor, or in terms of an actor's interpersonal perceptions. The twelve-year-olds usually gave explanations in psychological terms.

5

Aspects of Interaction Emphasized by the Children

To assess the aspects of the interaction the children talked about spontaneously, each episode was analyzed in terms of the points that *could* be mentioned. To obtain this model, two judges individually studied each of the five episodes of each movie and read the typed transcript of the dialogue and detailed action. In doing this, they took account of what the writer of the script and the characters in the action apparently intended to portray, of the way in which each turn in the unfolding drama set the stage for the next, and of how each successive sequence emerged from or was related to preceding events. The two judges had no difficulty in reaching consensus concerning what they regarded as the sequence of separately described events in each episode.

For this analysis, the judges in general tried to limit themselves to items that would be considered within the "reporting-describing" category of statements to see to what extent the children talked about overt action, verbal communication, expressive behavior, obvious feelings, and obvious intentions that were essential to an understanding of the drama and yet required no interpretation or inference.

An evaluation then was possible of the children's own accounts of what happened in the movies, in order to determine the frequency with which children at the three age levels spontaneously mentioned what the judges regarded as the main items — which items were mentioned most frequently and which items least frequently, which items that were considered important by adults were omitted entirely, and what kinds of errors in perception occurred.

A separate analysis was made of the content of the children's responses to the specific interview questions, to see to what extent the children could give "inferences-interpretations" about feelings, thoughts, and intentions when their attention was directed to these, and to see the content of the explanations given when they were specifically asked, "Why?"

The analyses of the spontaneous accounts and of the answers to the interview questions pointed up that relying only on a child's own narrative account of an episode would not adequately reflect the child's ability to perceive psychological material. Many times "psychological" aspects of interaction and explanations for the interaction, which were not mentioned by the children in giving their own accounts of what happened, were talked about in response to specific questioning. And even though the twelve-year-olds had more "psychological" interpretations than the six-year-olds, the older children, like the younger ones, tended to omit much that was mentioned when they specifically were asked "how" and "why" questions.

The aspects of interaction that seemed to be emphasized by the children in giving their own accounts of what happened were: the setting of an episode or the opening action of a scene; unusual or exciting events (such as a child riding on an elephant); and the gross overt action, rather than the nuances of interaction and of feelings and intentions that gave special meaning to the ongoing dramatic episode.

There was little spontaneous mention of the adults' feelings, intentions, and thoughts, though there was a developmental trend here, the nine-year-olds reporting the adults' actions and states of mind more often than the six-year-olds, and the twelve-year-olds reporting on them more often than the nine-year-olds. With age also there appeared to be more elaboration on the thoughts, perceptions, and expectations that accompany feelings for all the characters, and more explaining in terms of a person's goals rather than simply in terms of a person reacting to a situation.

The rest of this chapter presents, for Movie A and Movie B, the sequence of events agreed on by the two judges for each episode, followed by a detailed analysis of the spontaneous accounts of the children as to what happened in the episode, and their answers to the interview questions.

Movie A

Episode 1

In this scene a girl who is using her new roller skates does not give the little boy who is watching a turn. He calls her a pig, and during the arguing that follows, the girl's mother looks out the window and tells the girl to give the boy a turn. The girl calls the boy a tattletale and

41

tells him to go home. He threatens to tell on the girl again, and to prevent this she pushes him down.

All three age groups gave most frequent mention to the opening situation where the girl was using her roller skates and the boy wanted a turn, and to the final action of the girl pushing the boy down. In addition, most of the children in the two older groups and half of the six-year-olds reported that the boy called the girl a pig.

From an adult's point of view, the events that transpired between the beginning of the episode when the girl was skating and the end of the episode when the girl pushed the boy down make more understandable and justifiable the girl's act in pushing the boy down. However, these events were infrequently mentioned by the children, and particularly the six-year-olds.

None of the children in any of the age groups referred to the mother's feelings in giving their accounts of what happened. Yet in the structured interview, when they were questioned, "How do you think the mother felt when she looked out the window and said to let the boy have the skates?" 14 of the six-year-olds and 13 of the nine-year-olds said that the mother was mad or cross or upset about the fighting or wanted the children to stop arguing. Half of the twelve-year-olds also answered in this way, but half went beyond this and added that "the mother thought the girl should share" or that "she should take turns" or be fair or that "the mother was against the girl's selfishness."

Episode 2

At the beginning of this scene the boy tells the girl's father the girl won't give him a turn on the skates, and the mother and father talk together about who should spank the girl. When the father asks the girl why she didn't give the boy a turn, she says he called her a pig. The boy denies this and the girl calls him a liar. At this point the father says that unless the girl gives the boy a turn she will have to go to bed without supper. The girl takes off her skates and starts to go to bed without supper, explaining that her father told her if she went to bed without supper she didn't have to give the boy a turn on the skates. The father, however, takes the skates and gives them to the boy as a present from the girl, and then sends the girl to bed without supper.

A difference appeared between the adults and all three age groups in discussing the adults' intentions in this episode. According to adult viewers, one of the most significant developments in this episode occurred when the father and mother of the girl who did not yield her skates thought that their daughter should be punished, but each tried to evade responsibility for the punishment and tried to shift responsibility to the other. No children at the six-year level and only two or three at each of the two older levels referred to this in giving their own accounts of what happened in the movie. A difference appeared between the six-year-olds and the two older groups in answering questions about this. The father had used as his excuse the fact that his hand was too big. When the question was asked in the interview, "Why did the father say his hand was too big?" none of the six-year-olds answered in terms of the father wanting to avoid responsibility. Some gave literal answers, such as, "Well, it was too big because he was a man," or, "Well, his hand was big because he worked on a farm and he had to have big hands." However some of the six-year-olds and most of the nine-year-olds and twelve-year-olds answered in terms of the father not wanting to spank the girl or not wanting to hurt her. And a few of the two older groups answered in terms of the father's underlying motive of trying to avoid responsibility and/or trying to get the mother to take responsibility.

The mother used as her excuse the statement that she was busy making supper. When specifically questioned, "Why did the mother say she was busy making supper?" over half of the six-year-olds answered in literal terms, such as, "It was getting late and the family was hungry," or, "It was getting to be time to eat," or "There was something cooking on the stove and the mother had to look at it." In contrast, all except one of the nine-year-olds and one of the twelve-year-olds answered in terms of the mother not wanting to spank the child and/or recognized that it was an excuse to get the father to take the responsibility for discipline.

There was another conspicuous difference between the six-year-olds and the two older groups in giving their accounts of the misunderstanding between the girl and her father in this episode. According to the adult judges, an important element which lays the groundwork for what follows in other episodes is the fact that the girl thought that if she went to bed without supper she could keep her skates and that the father did not share this understanding but rather took the skates away, gave them to the boy as a present, and sent the girl to bed without supper. The two items mentioned most frequently by the six-year-olds were that the father took the skates from the girl and gave them to the boy and that the father sent the girl to bed, though even these most frequently mentioned items were mentioned by only about half of the six-year-olds. In contrast, the item mentioned most frequently by the two older groups was that the father *threatened* that unless the girl gave the boy a turn on the skates she would have to go to bed without supper. These two groups also frequently mentioned that the girl said her father had told her if she went to bed she didn't have to give the boy a turn on the skates.

Although on many items the big differences were between the six-year-olds and the two older groups, a difference appeared between the twelve-year-olds and the two younger groups with regard to the girl's feelings in this episode. When the children were questioned, "How do you think the girl felt when she took off the skates and said she was going to bed without any supper?" over half of the six-year-olds and many of the nine-year-olds answered that she was feeling mad, angry, and/or not wanting to give the skates to the boy. But almost half of the six-year-olds and almost half of the nine-year-olds said, "I don't know," or gave incorrect answers. In striking contrast, twelve of the twelve-year-olds answered at a complex level, saying such things as "The girl was satisfied about keeping the skates but sorry about missing supper," or, "The girl thought that in this way she would be able to keep the skates."

When the children were questioned, "How do you think the girl felt *after* the father gave the skates to the boy?" practically all of the six-year-olds and nine-year-olds answered correctly but simply that the girl felt sad, unhappy, sorry, hurt, or angry, whereas 15 of the twelve-year-olds answered at a complex level, saying that "the girl didn't want to give the skates as a present but had to" or that "she thought her father was unfair and mean" or that "she felt sorry *and* mad."

Episode 3

This scene opens with the father trying to read his newspaper but looking up frequently toward the girl's room. When the girl asks to kiss her father good night, however, he brusquely sends her back to bed. Obviously feeling uneasy and uncomfortable, he goes into the kitchen and says he is going outside. The mother then tells the father that a circus is passing through town and he thanks her.

One of the events mentioned most frequently by all three age groups was that the girl asked to kiss her father good night. However, a difference appeared between the twelve-year-olds and the two younger groups when the children were questioned, "Why did the girl ask to kiss her father good night?" Half of the six-year-olds and half of the nine-year-olds gave reasons such as, "Because she was lonely up there," or, "Because she was sorry," or, "Because she loved him." Some answered, "Because she wanted to get out of bed." On the other hand, 15 of the twelve-year-olds gave reasons such as, "Because she wanted to make up with her father," or, "Because she wanted to see if he was still mad at her," or, "Because she wanted her father to be nice to her again."

From an adult point of view, the most important elements in this episode are the father's discomfort over his relationship with his daughter, and the mother mentioning the circus as a way for the father to make up to his daughter for what had happened between them earlier. Again an impressive difference was apparent between the six-year-olds and the two older groups in mentioning anything about the grown-ups in this episode and in answering questions about them. None of the six-year-olds mentioned spontaneously the fact that the father was unable to concentrate on his newspaper and/or was thinking about what had happened earlier in the day, whereas a few nine-year-olds and half of the twelve-year-olds did. Only one of the six-year-olds mentioned that the father was feeling unhappy, whereas several nine-year-olds and over half of the twelve-year-olds noted this. Along with this, when the children were specifically questioned, "How do you think the father felt when the girl asked to kiss him good night?" none of the six-year-olds answered in terms of the father feeling sorry for the girl or sorry for what he had done or being confused or puzzled or pulled in two directions, while 12 of the nine-year-olds and 15 of the twelve-year-olds answered in this way.

In addition, only 6 of the six-year-olds mentioned that the mother talked about the circus to the father, whereas practically all of the nine-year-olds and twelve-year-olds mentioned it spontaneously. And when the children were asked, "Why did the mother mention the circus to the father?" 14 of the six-year-olds answered either, "I don't know," or gave explanations such as, "Because the mother wanted to go to the circus," or, "Because the mother thought the father would like the circus." In contrast, practically all of the nine-year-olds and the twelve-year-olds got the idea that the mother wanted the father to take his daughter to the circus.

Episode 4

At the beginning of this scene, the father and the girl are watching the circus trucks go past. When the trucks stop and the girl sees an elephant's head, she asks if the elephant will come out. Her father goes over and asks the driver. When the driver says no, the father offers to pay him. The driver asks for five dollars but the father has only four, which the driver takes. Returning to the girl, the father tells her the driver said he was always glad to show elephants to little girls. The elephant comes out and does tricks, and as she watches the little girl is very happy and excited. Seeing her enthusiasm, the driver offers her a ride on the elephant, and the girl is even more thrilled, though somewhat scared, while she is on the elephant.

The emphasis of the adult judges differed considerably from the emphasis of the nine- and twelve-year-olds, which in turn differed considerably from the emphasis of the six-year-olds.

The one item that was mentioned by all the six-year-olds, all except one nine-year-old and all except one twelve-year-old was that the girl got a ride on the elephant. Along with this, another frequently mentioned item was that the elephant did tricks.

According to the adult judges, an important element was that when the driver refused to take the elephant out of the truck the father offered to pay, and that when the father returned to the girl he concealed this, telling her instead that the driver was always glad to show elephants to little girls. The item *least* frequently mentioned by all three age groups was that the father told the girl the driver was always glad to show elephants to little girls. When the children were specifically questioned about *why* the father told his daughter the driver was always glad to show elephants to little girls, most of the six-year-olds said, "I don't know," or answered in terms of the driver offering to show the elephant, such as, "Because the driver liked little girls," or, "Because little girls like elephants." In contrast, half of the nine-year-olds and 16 of the twelve-year-olds got the idea that the father didn't want his daughter to know he had to pay to have the elephant brought out.

Other differences appeared between the six-year-olds and the two older groups. Nine of the nine-year-olds and 15 of the twelve-year-olds mentioned that the driver refused to take the elephant out and that the father offered to pay, but only 2 of the six-year-olds noted this. Along this same line, when the children were questioned about *why* the father asked the driver to take the elephant out of the truck, most of the nine-year-olds and twelve-year-olds gave answers such as, "The father wanted to make the little girl happy," or, "The father didn't want the little girl to feel disappointed [unhappy]," while only 5 of the six-year-olds answered in this way. When the question was raised, "Why did the man ask the girl if she would like to take a ride on the elephant?" many of the six-year-olds gave answers such as, "Because the girl had a nice dress on," or, "'Because elephants like to have girls on their trunks," or, "Elephants are for rides," while 13 of the nine-year-olds and all except 2 of the twelve-year-olds answered in terms of the driver responding to the girl's enthusiasm.

Episode 5

This scene shows the father and daughter, both obviously happy and content, driving home. When the girl asks her father if she can kiss him good night this time, he says yes. She says she is sorry about the afternoon, and then says it has been the happiest summer of her life. He says there will be more and then kisses her.

There were suggestive differences between the six-year-olds and the two older groups in what was spontaneously mentioned and in how the interview questions were answered. In giving their own accounts of what happened, the children in general gave little mention to the feelings of either the girl or the father. Yet, when they were specifically questioned in the interview, "How do you think the girl felt as she and her father were driving home?" practically all of the children answered that she was happy, and a few of the two older groups added that the girl now knew her father likes her or mentioned feelings about the afternoon or about her father. Also, when they were questioned, "How do you think the father felt as they were driving home?" practically all of the children answered that he was happy and some of the two older groups added that "he was glad he had made up for the afternoon" or that "he was glad that he and his daughter were friends again."

Going beyond this, when the children were asked *why* the girl felt happy, practically all of the six-year-olds and the majority of the nine-year-olds and twelve-year-olds gave answers such as, "Because she had a good time," or, "Because she saw the elephant," or, "Because she saw the circus." A few of the older groups referred in some way to the girl making up with her father or something about her relationship with her father. When they were asked *why* the father felt happy, many of the six-year-olds gave answers such as, "Because he had fun at the circus," or, "Because he saw the elephant," the same kinds of explanations that were given for the girl feeling happy. Eleven of the six-year-olds, 16 of the nine-year-olds, and 16 of the twelve-year-olds answered, "Because his daughter was happy," or, "Because his daughter saw the elephant," or, "Because his daughter had fun." A few of the two older groups and one of the six-year-olds referred to the father-daughter relationship.

Most of the children in all three age groups reported that the girl asked if her father would kiss her good night. But the one event in this episode that was mentioned *more frequently* by the six-year-olds than by the two older groups was the fact that the father *did* kiss the girl good night.

Movie B

Episode 1

This scene opens with a boy and girl walking along a road, talking about what they are going to be. When the boy says he will be a

47

soldier and have a gun, the girl says she will be a WAC and shoot more because she is older. He says girls can't shoot. At that moment they see a squirrel and to show the boy how she will shoot, the girl throws a rock at the squirrel and kills it. She cries and says she didn't mean to kill the squirrel. The boy tells her red squirrels are bad, but she says this squirrel wasn't doing anything bad.

An impressive difference became obvious between the children's comments and those of adults in talking about this episode. One of the events singled out for most frequent mention by *all* three age groups was that the girl threw a rock that killed the squirrel. From an adult point of view the interchange between the boy and girl is important because it was after the boy said that girls can't shoot that the girl threw the rock at the squirrel and killed it. This makes "understandable" the girl being provoked to throw the rock. However, the fact that the boy said girls can't shoot was the *least* frequently mentioned item by all three age groups. And in fact, there was little or no mention by the six-year-olds of any of the interaction leading to the girl's throwing the rock, though there was rather frequent mention by the two older groups that the boy talked about being a soldier and the girl said she would be a WAC.

As with Movie A, differences appeared between the six-year-olds and the two older age groups in giving explanations. In the interview, when the children were specifically questioned, "Why did the girl throw the rock?" half of the six-year-olds either answered, "I don't know," or gave answers such as, "Because it was a bad squirrel," or, "Because the girl thought the squirrel was going to bite her." In contrast, all except one nine-year-old and all except one twelve-year-old answered in terms of the girl pretending to be a soldier or pretending to shoot, and a few of these older children even explained that "the girl wanted to show the boy that girls can shoot as good as boys."

In addition, little mention was made by the six-year-olds that the girl said she didn't mean to kill the squirrel and that the boy said red squirrels are bad, while considerable mention was made of these two elements by the older groups. On the other hand, although only one six-year-old spontaneously mentioned that the girl was unhappy, when the children were questioned in the interview, "How do you think the girl felt after she threw the rock?" 19 used words such as "sad," "sorry," "unhappy." Most of the nine-year-olds and twelve-year-olds also answered in this way, but a few went beyond this to say that "the girl probably wished she didn't throw the rock" or "the girl probably wouldn't ever do anything like that again."

When questioned even further, "Why did the girl cry after the rock hit the squirrel?" most of the six-year-olds gave answers in terms of the existing situation, such as, "Because the squirrel was dead," whereas most of the two older groups answered in psychological terms, such as, "Because she was sorry that she had killed it," or, "Because she thought she really did bad," or, "Because she didn't want to hurt it."

Episode 2

In this scene the mother tells the children to ring the dinner bell and get washed. There is a brief argument about who can pull the bell, and the boy wins. Then the children pump water for each other and wash. As they are washing, the mother tells the girl to wash her face. The girl says she didn't touch anything with her face but then washes it.

A difference between the six-year-olds and the two older groups in terms of the emphasis upon overt action is indicated by the fact that the one item mentioned more frequently by the six-year-olds than by the nine-year-olds and twelve-year-olds was that the boy rang the dinner bell. This item was the least frequently mentioned by the two older groups.

As was already indicated many times, a psychological detail that was not mentioned in the spontaneous account *was* given in response to a specific question. For example, none of the children talked about the girl's feelings with regard to the fact that the boy rang the dinner bell. Yet when the question was asked, "How do you think the girl felt about the boy ringing the dinner bell?" the majority of the six-year-olds and nine-year-olds answered that the girl didn't like it or that she was sad or that she wanted to do it. The twelve-year-olds went beyond this, 16 of them stating that "the girl wanted to ring it but thought that since the boy was the guest he should" or "the girl was giving in to what had to be."

Adults were amused by the girl's statement that she didn't need to wash her face because she didn't touch anything with her face. This was the least frequently mentioned item by the six-year-olds for this episode, and only half of each of the older groups mentioned it and indicated in some way that they thought it was funny.

Episode 3

At the beginning of this scene, the father is coming home and the children run over to him. The girl asks if squirrels are bad and talks about the bad things squirrels do. At first the father says he doesn't mind squirrels, but then, noticing the girl's sad expression, he asks her, "What's the matter?" She tells him about killing the squirrel. He then says there is a present in the barn for her.

An important part of this episode, according to adult judges, is that the girl tells the father about killing the squirrel and that he first tries to reassure her and then, seeing he is unsuccessful, he mentions something in the barn as a way of trying to take her mind off the killing. The children of all three age groups, however, highlighted the beginning and the end — that the father came home and the children joined him and that the father said he had a present in the barn for the girl — and for the most part ignored the interaction in the middle part. The six-year-olds neglected the entire conversation in which the girl was talking to her father about the squirrel. The nine-year-olds and twelve-year-olds noted that the girl told her father about killing the squirrel but gave much less mention to the rest of the conversation. The item *least* frequently mentioned by all three age groups was that the father asked the girl, "What's the matter?" after he noticed her sadness.

Differences between the six-year-olds and the two older groups also appeared in answer to the interview questions. When specifically asked, "Why did the girl talk about the squirrel being bad?" 11 of the six-year-olds either answered, "I don't know," or gave answers in terms of squirrels being bad, such as, "Because squirrels eat things," or, "Because squirrels bite," or, "Because the squirrel was red." In contrast, most of the nine-year-olds and twelve-year-olds answered in terms of the girl's interest or concern, stating, "Because she wanted to know if they were really bad," or, "Because the boy said red squirrels are bad," or, "Because she wanted to know if they are bad so that if the squirrel was bad it wouldn't matter if she killed it."

The children were also asked, "Why did the father ask, 'What's the matter?' after he said he didn't mind the squirrels getting a square meal?" Nine of the six-year-olds either said, "I don't know," or answered in terms of the squirrel, such as, "Because he thought the squirrel was stealing," or answered in terms of the father knowing about something that he didn't find out about until later in the episode, i.e., "Because the girl killed the squirrel." Most of the nine-year-olds and twelve-year-olds said it was "because the girl kept talking about the squirrel" or "because the girl kept asking questions about red squirrels," or went even further in terms of the father's inner thoughts or the father's perception of the girl, giving answers such as, "Because the father thought something was wrong because the girl talked about squirrels," or, "Because he saw that she looked so sad and she was asking so many questions," or, "Because he thought there was something behind her questioning."

Again in this episode a "psychological" detail that was not mentioned in the spontaneous account was given in response to specific questioning. *None* of the children had spontaneously mentioned the father's feelings in giving their own accounts of what happened. When they were asked, however, "How do you think the father felt after he heard about the squirrel?" practically all of the children said he was sad. A few of the twelve-year-olds went beyond this to say that "the father was feeling sorry for his daughter" or that "he wanted to make his daughter feel better."

A big difference appeared between the six-year-olds and the two older groups in accounting for the father's actions. When the children were specifically asked in the interview, "Why did the father say he had a present for the girl?" the majority of the six-year-olds either said, "I don't know," or answered in terms of some reason irrelevant to what they had observed in the film, for example, "Because she was good," "Because he was nice," or, "Because he *did* have a present." About half of each of the two older groups explained it in terms of his concern for his daughter, stating it was "because she felt bad" or "because he wanted to make her happy" or "because he wanted to make her feel better." And almost half of each of the two older groups explained it in terms of the father empathizing with the daughter, as for instance, stating, "Because he knew how she felt because of the squirrel and he knew this would make her a little happier," or, "Because he wanted to take her mind off the squirrel and to keep her from being so upset about killing it." None of the six-year-olds answered in this way.

Episode 4

In this scene the girl sees that her present is a newborn calf. She asks if it is her own and her father says it is. She then asks if the calf was born at the time she was killing the squirrel and the father says it probably was. During this time the boy is asking how the calf will get dry if the mother keeps licking it and commenting that the calf sure is wet.

As indicated previously, the children tended to mention the gross, overt action more than the nuances of interaction, and this was brought out clearly in talking about this episode. The item mentioned most frequently by *all* the age groups was that the girl saw that her present was a newborn calf. But even this was mentioned by only half the six-year-olds. For the most part, the six-year-olds did not mention any of the other main points about this episode. The nine-year-olds and the twelve-year-olds, to some extent, reported that the girl asked if the calf was her own and the father said it was, and that the boy asked how the calf would ever get dry if the mother kept licking it. However, few of the nine-year-olds and the twelve-year-olds, and none of the six-year-olds, spontaneously mentioned that the girl asked if the calf was born at the time she was killing the squirrel and that the father said it probably was.

Questioning about this episode brought out some differences between the nine-year-olds and twelve-year-olds, as well as between the six-year-olds and the nine-year-olds. When the children were asked, "Why did the girl ask if the calf was born at the time she was killing the squirrel?" the six-year-olds could not give adequate answers, and practically all of them answered, "I don't know," or, "Just because . . . ," or, "Because she was not there when he was born." The majority of the nine-year-olds answered in obvious ways, stating it was "because she wondered" or "because she wanted to know," while the majority of the twelve-year-olds gave explanations such as, "She wanted to know if something good was happening while she was doing something bad," or, "She wanted to replace what is dead by something alive," or, "She wanted to balance something dead by something just born."

There was also an impressive difference between the twelve-year-olds and the two younger age groups in answering the question, "How do you think the boy felt while he was looking at the calf?" The majority of the six-year-olds and nine-year-olds either said they did not know or mentioned a simple and incorrect feeling, such as that the boy was angry, mad, or sad. Practically all of the twelve-year-olds, however, answered in terms of the boy's inner thoughts or a complicated feeling, such as, "The boy wished he had a calf," or, "He was puzzled why the mother cow was licking it," or, "He was jealous that the girl did something wrong and then sort of got a prize."

Episode 5

This scene opens with the family eating. After the girl asks if she can feed her calf, the boy says if he had a calf it would be bigger than the girl's. The mother says the calf is just "pretend" the girl's. Taken aback, the girl says her father didn't say that. He agrees he didn't say it, but says maybe the mother is right. The girl is obviously sad and the mother, seeing the girl's expression, says maybe it is best for the girl to have the calf.

This episode pointed up the greater similarity between the twelve-year-olds and adults, and the differences between the twelve-year-olds and the two younger groups. From an adult point of view, one of the most important elements in the episode was that the father admitted he had not said the calf was just "pretend" the girl's but then hurried to say that maybe the mother was right in saying so. This was mentioned by only about half of the six-year-olds and about half of the nine-year-olds, but was mentioned by all the twelve-year-olds except one. Then, when the children were specifically asked in the interview, "How do you think the father felt when he said maybe the mother was right?" the six-year-olds and the nine-year-olds responded mainly to his facial expression and more often answered just that he felt sad or unhappy or bad or sorry, while the twelve-year-olds more often put themselves into the situation and imagined a more total response, such as, "He was ashamed because he had given something to her and then taken it back like an Indian giver," or, "He didn't want to say the mother was all wrong and that he was all right, but he also didn't want to hurt the girl's feelings."

In addition, this episode pointed to some of the differences between the adults and the children. Another important development from an adult point of view was that after the mother said the calf was just "pretend" the girl's and saw the girl's reaction to this statement, the mother changed her mind and said maybe it was best for the girl to have the calf. The children reported primarily on what was said and did not report on the psychological aspects, such as the girl's reaction and the mother's observation of the girl's feelings. The children noted the initial mention by the mother that the calf was just "pretend" the girl's, this being one of the most frequently mentioned items for all three age groups for this episode. They also noted that at the end of the episode the mother said maybe it was best for the girl to have the calf, this being mentioned by most of the nine-year-olds and twelve-year-olds and by about half of the six-year-olds. But there was less mention by the children of the girl's reaction to the mother, and the item mentioned *least* frequently by all three age groups was that the mother saw the girl's sad expression.

However, the children were better able to report on these aspects when they were specifically questioned. When asked, "Why did the mother change her mind about the calf?" 8 of the six-year-olds, 14 of the nine-year-olds, and 18 of the twelve-year-olds answered in terms of the mother's perception of the girl, such as stating it was "because she saw the effect on the girl when she said the calf wasn't hers" or "because she saw that taking the calf away was worse than she thought."

Errors in Perception

The protocols were also examined to discover whether there were errors in perception, and if so, the kinds of errors that occurred. Each protocol was read through in its entirety and the errors marked. This included distorting what was said, either by including statements that were not made or by twisting what was said so as to give a different meaning; distorting what was done, either by seeing actions that did not take place or misperceiving what did happen; and misperceptions of the relationships of the people interacting in the movie.

Though the six-year-olds as a group made somewhat more errors than the nine-year-olds and the twelve-year-olds, and the nine-year-olds made somewhat more errors than the twelve-year-olds, the differences were so small as not to be statistically significant. The average per child for each age group was about one or two for each of the movies.

For each movie there were two to four children in each age group who misperceived the relationship of the children. They overlooked cues such as the boy insisting on ringing the dinner bell because "I'm the guest" and thought the boy was the girl's brother.

At times the children reported dialogue that did not occur or action that did not occur but that certainly was implied. For example, in Movie A, when the mother and father were talking about how to discipline the girl for not sharing her roller skates, several children reported, incorrectly, that the mother said, "Why don't you spank her?" Or, as another example, when the father was distraught about not kissing the girl good night, some of the children reported, incorrectly, that he tore up the newspaper he was looking at. Also, some of the children reported, incorrectly, that the girl had asked for a ride on the elephant. Examples in Movie B included reporting, incorrectly, that the girl picked up a rock and threw it at the squirrel, though actually she was carrying the rock in her hand; or reporting, incorrectly, that at the pump the boy said, "Let me wash first," when actually the girl had told him to be the first to wash.

Sometimes a child would complete a story to get closure by mentioning actions that didn't happen but certainly could reasonably follow, such as, "After they washed they went into the house." Or, a child might fill out details to make a whole picture, such as, "The girl was still skating while the boy was talking to her father." Among the older children, there was some extrapolating from a character's reaction, such as, "She probably never saw an elephant before," or, "She probably never had a pet." Also, an older child sometimes tried to account for behavior in a reasonable way by taking another's role and probable definition of the situation, saying, for instance, "The mother hadn't seen what happened and didn't know and that is why she said that."

Summary

In the present sample, children at the six-year level, the nine-year level, and the twelve-year level seemed to be more oriented toward the overt, factual, and literal than toward "psychological content" when giving an account of an interpersonal incident, though they were able to talk about the latter when specifically questioned. Many times a "psychological" detail was not mentioned when the child gave her own account of what happened but was presented in a plausible manner in response to a question. The tendency not to mention the psychological aspects of the interaction appeared not only in connection with intentions that were portrayed but also in connection with obvious and explicit expressions of feelings, such as anger, sadness, and fear. This would suggest that the apparent literal-mindedness, especially in the older children, does not occur because of lack of perceptiveness or lack of the ability to perceive feelings and intentions, but rather reflects a tendency to communicate in a factual, reporting style. The children do not seem spontaneously to direct much attention to psychological content when giving their version of what occurs in an interpersonal setting.

Differences of *all* kinds were more apparent between the six-year-olds and the two older groups than between the nine-year-olds and the twelve-year-olds, though some differences between the latter also appeared. One of the big differences between the younger and the two older age groups was in reporting about the adult's actions and states of mind. The older two groups more often mentioned the feelings and thoughts of the father and mother and the communications of the father and the mother. Also, they were more likely to answer questions about the feelings and intentions of the adults, while the six-year-olds more often said, "I don't know."

Differences appeared also in the way the children answered questions about feelings. Many times, children of all three age groups reported that anger or hurt or happiness was being expressed, but usually only the older children went beyond this to elaborate on accompanying thoughts or expectations or perceptions. For example, when the boy lied and said he did not call the girl a pig, most of the six-year-olds reported that the girl felt mad or angry or frustrated, as did the older children, but six children in each of the older two groups added that she anticipated getting into trouble and/or wanted revenge. The six-year-olds described the characters more often as just reacting with feelings, while the older children described them as more actively thinking and planning their actions and as having goals in mind.

Among all three age groups, there were relatively few errors in perception. Usually what was reported was accurate. But much that was considered essential by adult judges was not mentioned by the children in their spontaneous accounts.

6

Evaluation of the Study

The findings of this study in general are in keeping with analogous findings that have emerged from other studies of children. However, some new dimensions are added that point the direction for future research.

In the present study, when children at the six-year level reported largely in situational terms and in terms of a literal repetition of the dialogue, it appeared that they were responding with thinking corresponding to Piaget's perceptual mode. There was much less of this at the nine- and twelve-year levels.

The fact that statements involving interpretations of feelings, inferences of thoughts, and inferences of intentions appeared hardly at all at the six-year level but appeared in statements of many of the nine-year-olds and twelve-year-olds, suggests a parallel between the findings of this study and Piaget's concept of egocentricity. According to Piaget, older children are more capable of viewing situations from the standpoint of the other person.

In line with this, it might be expected that nine- and twelve-year-olds would be able to talk about another person's behavior, thoughts, and feelings from the standpoint of that other person to a greater extent than would be true of the more egocentrically oriented six-year-olds. The present study found that in giving their own accounts of what happened the older two groups more often than the six-year-olds did mention the feelings, thoughts, and perceptions of the grown-ups, and that in answering questions about feelings or intentions, the older children elaborated more in terms of the person's thoughts, perceptions, and expectations.

Also, in keeping with Piaget's work, the six-year-olds in this study offered causal explanations less often than the nine-year-olds and twelve-year-olds, and their explanations were almost always in situational rather than psychological terms. However, the finding that about half of the six-year-olds in the present study used explanatory statements suggests the possibility that six-year-olds can apply the concept of causation in their observation of human behavior more readily than in dealing with abstract and impersonal logical problems.

According to the present findings, in giving their spontaneous reports younger children generally talked less than the older children about intentions, and when specifically questioned about intentions the six-year-olds frequently could not answer, saying, "I don't know." When they fail to talk in terms of intentions, it perhaps means they do not think in terms of intentions. This would be in keeping with Piaget's view of moral judgment, that they do not judge in terms of intentions.

As mentioned in Chapter I, studies of perception indicated that with increasing age children structure their percepts along less literal lines and omit irrelevant details. The present study also found that the six-year-olds answered questions in literal terms and that, in giving their own accounts of what happened, they mentioned details that were irrelevant (as judged by adults) more frequently than did the nine- or twelve-year-olds.

Just as previous studies of social development found a change with age, so did the present study. The order of development did *not* appear to be a haphazard one. Rather, certain general trends appeared. The present findings indicate that children are likely to make statements that report the objective situation-action and the dialogue before they make statements that explain sequences of behavior. The findings also indicate that explanatory statements are likely to occur before inferring-interpreting kinds of statements are made. In trying to explain, children at the youngest level made their explanations predominantly in situational terms. Explanation in psychological terms appears to be a later development, followed by explanations in terms of interpersonal perceptions.

According to the present results, children, in making inferences-interpretations, apparently infer thoughts and/or intentions before feelings and infer feelings before they infer interpersonal perceptions. Gollin, whose work was cited in Chapter I, has concluded that the use of inference in interpreting observed behavior is a relatively late developmental phenomenon. But the present study found there was some inferring among the six-year-olds, although there was significantly more among the nine-year-olds and the twelve-year-olds.

Limitations of the Study

In presenting sound films portraying ongoing social interaction, the present study made the assumption that the kinds of social interaction presented for the child's observation approximated, to a large extent, the kinds of interaction the child normally come in contact with. It was also assumed that the task required of the child in giving an account of what happened and in answering questions in the interview approximated the situation a child faces when he is asked in everyday life to tell about something he has observed. These assumptions seem plausible; to verify them would require a separate study.

Another assumption of the present study was that to a large extent what a child says about an observed episode of social interaction gives some indication of what she has seen and understood. However, what children say does not necessarily define the limits of their understanding.[1] In the present study, the child was provided standard situations in which she was asked to demonstrate her understanding of social interaction. The investigator realized it was not possible to know what the child was aware of but only what the child reported. And frequently the child recalled and reported details when questioned about "how" and "why" that she omitted in giving her own spontaneous account of what happened. In other words, many of the omissions in the spontaneous accounts were not due to failure to notice the details but the failure to mention them.

In real-life situations children often show sensitivity to the moods and feelings of adults and other children.[2] They pick up many subtle aspects of a social situation and act upon them. Yet they may not be able to talk freely about them.

The fact that a child in reporting an episode does not mention a

---

[1] In many ways this is analogous to the problem that arises in measuring general intelligence. In assessing intelligence, the test situation attempts to provide standard situations in which intelligent behavior can be observed. The tester can only work with what is expressed by the child. The child may be more intelligent than the test shows, since many other factors may enter into the test situation. Therefore, it can only be stated, as many testers have done, that the "child is *at least* this intelligent," though the child may be more intelligent than comes out in the testing situation. Intelligence is inferred from the overt behavior but the tester realizes there may be more than is being expressed.

[2] One of the preliminary steps in the project dealing with children's awareness of and insight into their own and others' thoughts, feelings, and intentions, conducted by Jersild and the present writer, was to collect several hundred anecedotal accounts of children's seemingly spontaneous reactions of this kind. These anecdotes, which, of course, have to be verified by more systematic inquiry, suggest that at least some children seem to have a remarkable degree of sensitivity to and awareness of other persons' states of mind even while they are still at an immature stage of thinking as judged by the criteria used in Piaget's studies.

specific psychological aspect, such as a feeling or an intention, may be due to any number of reasons. She may not have perceived what happened. She may have perceived it and may have the language to talk about it but may think that what she saw is not important enough to mention. Or she may have perceived it and may have the language to talk about it but, based on earlier experiences, think that this is something she should not talk about.

Indications for Further Research

One of the problems for future research is to evolve ways of getting closer to what the young children are actually responding to and of getting beyond just what children say. This might be through a system of more intensive probing, or by having the child draw pictures to express what cannot be expressed in words, or by requiring the child actually to respond by action in a given situation.

The most conspicuous developmental increases occurred between six and nine years, suggesting that this period represents an important transitional phase. Further studies might indicate to what extent certain changes can be pinpointed at the seven- or eight-year level and in what ways the developmental trend continues beyond the twelve-year level into adolescence. Also, since there were no differences between the six-year-olds and the two older groups in most of the "reporting-describing" categories, it would be interesting to lower the age limit in future investigations to see whether there is a difference between the proportion who report on the situation-action and the verbal communication and the proportion who report on obvious feelings and intentions. It would also be of interest to compare boys with girls to see whether the same developmental trends appear, and whether they occur at the same ages; and to compare children of different intelligence levels and of different socioeconomic backgrounds.

Further studies might also be done to investigate whether development could be influenced by special instruction. According to the theory underlying the larger project of which this study was a part, children and youth have more capacity for understanding their own and others' feelings and motives than has generally been acknowledged.[3] Foote and Cottrell have discussed this as an aspect of interpersonal competence and have also suggested that it could be cultivated through planned educational experiences.[4]

[3] A. T. Jersild, "Self-understanding in childhood and adolescence," *Amer. Psychologist,* VI (1951), 122–26.

[4] N. N. Foote and L. S. Cottrell, Jr., *Identity and interpersonal competence: A new direction in family research* (Chicago: Univ. of Chicago Press, 1955).

Several unhypothesized results appeared in the present study that could be tested in other investigations. There appeared to be an increase with age in the ability to talk about the communications of adults and about the feelings and intentions of adults. In addition, there appeared to be more elaboration on the thoughts, perceptions, and expectations that accompany feelings, and there appeared to be more describing and explaining in terms of a person's goals, whereas younger children appeared to describe and explain more in terms of a person reacting to a situation.

7

Summary

The purpose of this study was to investigate children's ability to describe and make inferences about feelings, thoughts, and intentions that occur in interpersonal relationships and their ability to account for the sequences of behavior that occur. The initial problem of finding an appropriate technique was resolved, after extensive exploration, by using sound films portraying episodes of social interaction suitable for presentation to children at various age levels and for eliciting children's own accounts of what had happened and their responses to a series of specific questions.

Method

Subjects

This research was carried out as a cross-sectional study, using 20 children at each of three age levels: six years, nine years, and twelve years. So that a small number of cases could be used most effectively, the subjects were limited to girls of average intelligence in a middle-class neighborhood.

Filmed Episodes of Social Interaction for Observation

Following preliminary exploration and experimentation, two movie excerpts depicting social interaction were selected from the commercial film *Our Vines Have Tender Grapes*. Each of the excerpts, referred to as Movie A and Movie B, represented a complete dramatic interlude, one episode leading to the next and reaching a climax in the manner of a finished story. Each movie portrayed a variety of feelings, a variety of motivations, a variety of family relationships, and a variety of social situations.

By dividing each movie into five episodes, it was possible to present a uniform sequence of stimulus situations to all children with a minimum strain on the child's ability to concentrate or to remember.

Movie A presents a story in which a father punishes a young girl for not sharing her new roller skates with a neighbor boy. However, he then feels conflict about the harshness of the punishment and seeks to "make up" for it by taking the girl to see a circus passing through town. In Movie B, the girl is upset because she has accidentally killed a squirrel. Her father gives her a calf for her own as a way of taking her mind off the squirrel. The mother says it is just "pretend" her calf, but then seeing the girl's disappointment decides it may be a good thing for her to have a calf of her own.

Interview Based on Sound Films

The movies were presented in a standard viewing situation, one movie being shown on each of two days a week apart. The children were interviewed individually, half seeing Movie A first and half seeing Movie B first.

After each episode, the film was stopped and the child was given a general instruction, "Pretend I didn't see the movie and tell me what happened," and her account was recorded verbatim. Following this, the child was asked a number of specific questions focused on how a character in the sound film felt, why he said what he did, or why he acted as he did.

Children's Own Accounts of What Happened

The children's own accounts of what happened in the movie were analyzed in terms of a set of three major categories, built upon what the children actually said: (1) reporting-describing, (2) explaining, and (3) inferring-interpreting. Each of these categories was further divided into subcategories.

For example, included within the category of reporting-describing were statements that reported on the setting in which the action took place; statements that described the overt action that occurred; statements that reported on expressive behavior such as crying or laughing; statements that mentioned feelings that were specifically mentioned in the dialogue or were obviously manifested by the expressive behavior or the action; and statements that mentioned intentions that were specifically mentioned in the dialogue or were obviously manifested by the action.

Within the category of explaining were included statements that gave an explanation of the observation in terms of the overt action that had occurred, the objective situation, or the dialogue; statements that gave an explanation of the interaction in terms of an actor's feelings, intentions, or thoughts; and statements that gave an explanation of the ongoing action in terms of one actor's perception of another actor's feelings, intentions, or thoughts.

The inferring-interpreting category was divided into four subcategories: statements that inferred or interpreted feelings not obviously expressed and not specifically labelled; statements that inferred intentions not obviously expressed and not specifically labelled; statements that inferred thoughts or expectations; and statements that inferred or interpreted an interpersonal perception by one actor of another actor's feelings, intentions, or thoughts.

Developmental Trends

Certain general developmental trends appeared in describing episodes of social interaction. With increase in age there were more children who gave causal explanations. Also, with age there was an increase in the number of children who made interpretations of feelings or who inferred thoughts and intentions not obviously expressed or specifically labeled. Development seemed to progress from describing a situation and/or reporting the overt action and dialogue to attempting to account for what had taken place in the social interaction by giving an explanation and then to inferring thoughts, intentions and feelings that were not obviously expressed or interpreting what was expressed on some "deeper" level.

There was a shift in the kinds of explanations given. At the six-year level explanations were primarily in terms of the situation in which the interaction took place, whereas with age there were more explanations in psychological terms, that is, in terms of a person's feelings or motives or thoughts and more explanations in terms of one actor responding to his perception of a co-actor's feelings or thoughts.

In addition, there was a shift with age in the kinds of inferences and interpretations that were made. Inferences about an actor's thoughts and/or his intentions appeared earlier than inferences about or interpretations of an actor's feelings. And interpretations of feelings appeared earlier than inferences about one actor's perceptions of another actor's psychological state.

Wherever there were statistically significant differences between the six-year-olds and the twelve-year-olds, there were also statistically significant differences between the six-year-olds and the nine-year-olds. Though there were not statistically significant differences between the

63

nine-year-olds and the twelve-year-olds, there did appear to be a progression from six years to nine years and from nine years to twelve years.

Children's Responses to Interview Questions

The children's responses to the specific interview questions were scored on a three-point scale — 0, 1, 2 — which was developed by adult judges after observing the film and analyzing the typed transcript. A score of "0" was given when the child said, "I don't know," or gave a response contradictory to the adult judges' consensus. A score of "1" was given to a response that was correct but mentioned a feeling that was specifically labeled or obviously portrayed in the film or a response that was correct but offered an explanation in terms of the objective situation or the overt action. A score of "2" was given to a response that mentioned a feeling or thought not obviously expressed, a complex combination of feelings or thoughts, or an explanation in psychological rather than situational terms.

Twenty-eight questions were asked about Movie A, which meant a total score of 56 was possible; and twenty-five questions were asked about Movie B, which meant a total score of 50 was possible.

Developmental Trends

The differences between the mean scores on both Movie A and Movie B at the three age levels were statistically significant at the .01 level. The children's answers to the interview questions showed a developmental trend, becoming less literal in the interpretations of what was said and done and showing more differentiation of interpretations of feelings, thoughts, and intentions.

In answering questions that called for *explanations* of behavior, there was a progression with age from saying they did not know or giving answers not appropriate to the action of the film or explaining an antecedent action by something that happened subsequently, to giving explanations in terms of the existing situation or the just-preceding action, to giving explanations in psychological terms, such as imputing motives, thoughts, or anticipations to an actor, or in terms of an actor's perceptions of a fellow actor's feelings or thoughts.

In answering questions about *feelings*, the children progressed with age from saying they did not know or mentioning a feeling that did not agree with the adult consensus, to reporting obvious, uncomplicated feelings mentioned in the dialogue or clearly presented in the action, to answering more in terms of complex combinations of feelings, inferring feelings not explicit in the dialogue or action, or naming a feeling and then elaborating in terms of the actor's thoughts, intentions, or expectations.

Aspects of Interaction Emphasized

A content analysis of the children's own accounts of what happened was made in order to ascertain the aspects of social interaction the children spontaneously talked about. In addition, a separate analysis was made of the content of the responses to the interview questions in order to ascertain to what extent the children could give interpretations or inferences regarding feelings, thoughts, and intentions when their attention was directed to specific actions in movies that portrayed, but did not explicitly identify, feelings, thoughts, and intentions, and to note the kinds of explanations children give when specifically asked why the characters in the movie acted or spoke as they did.

Developmental Trends

All the children, but especially the six-year-olds, tended to mention the gross, overt actions of each episode more than the nuances of interaction and of feelings and intentions that gave special meaning to the ongoing dramatic episode. There also appeared to be a tendency to mention the setting of a scene or the opening action of a scene and to mention the more dramatic happenings.

The six-year-olds seemed to describe the characters more often as just reacting with feelings, while the older children seemed to describe them as more actively thinking and having goals in mind.

Frequently "psychological" details not mentioned when the children gave their own accounts of what happened were dealt with effectively when the children were asked specific questions. Even when able to perceive feelings and intentions, children in this study tended to emphasize the factual and literal rather than the psychological content of what was portrayed.

There was a substantial difference between the six-year-olds and the older children in reporting about the adults' actions and states of mind, the older two groups more often mentioning the communications, feelings, and thoughts of the adults and more often being able to answer specific questions about the feelings and intentions of the adults.

Conclusion

The most conspicuous developmental increases of all kinds occurred in the age interval from six to nine, suggesting that this period, or part of it, represents an important transitional phase in the aspect of development here being studied.

APPENDIX A

1. INTERVIEW QUESTIONS

For Movie A, twenty-eight questions were formulated:

Episode 1

1. Why do you think the boy called the girl a pig?
2. How do you think the mother felt when she looked out the window and said to let the boy have the skates?
3. Why do you think the girl pushed the boy down?

Episode 2

4. When the father and mother were talking together, why do you think the father said his hand was too big?
5. Why do you think the mother said she was busy making supper?
6. How do you think the girl felt when the boy lied and said he didn't call her a pig?
7. How do you think the girl felt when she took off the skates and said she was going to bed without any supper?
8. Why do you think the father gave the skates to the boy?
9. How do you think the girl felt after he gave the skates to the boy?
10. How do you think the father felt after he gave the skates to the boy and after the girl went into the house?
11. How do you think the boy felt after the father gave him the skates?

Episode 3

12. At the beginning, why do you think the father kept looking up instead of reading his newspaper?
13. Why do you think the girl asked to kiss her father good night?
14. How do you think the father felt when the girl asked to kiss him good night?
15. Why do you think the father said he was going to take a bath?
16. Why do you think the mother mentioned the circus to the father?
17. How do you think the father felt after she mentioned the circus?

Episode 4

18. Why do you think the father asked the driver to take the elephant out of the truck?

66

19. Why do you think the father told his daughter the driver was always glad to show elephants to little girls?
20. Why do you think the man asked the girl if she would like to take a ride on the elephant?
21. How do you think the girl felt while she was on the elephant?
22. How do you think the father felt while the girl was on the elephant?

Episode 5

23. How do you think the girl felt as she and her father were driving home?
24. Why do you think the girl felt happy?
25. Why do you think the girl asked if she could kiss her father good night this time?
26. How do you think the father felt as they were driving home?
27. Why do you think the father felt happy?
28. Why do you think the father said there would be more nice things happening to her?

For Movie B, twenty-five questions were formulated:

Episode 1

1. Why do you think the boy said his father killed all the buffalo?
2. Why do you think the girl threw the rock?
3. How do you think the girl felt after she threw the rock?
4. Why do you think the girl cried after the rock hit the squirrel?
5. Why do you think the boy said red squirrels are bad?

Episode 2

6. How do you think the girl felt about the boy ringing the dinner bell?
7. How do you think the girl felt when her mother told her to wash her face?
8. How do you think the mother felt after the girl said she didn't touch anything with her face?

Episode 3

9. Why do you think the girl talked about squirrels being bad?
10. Why do you think the father asked, "What's the matter?" after he said he didn't mind the squirrels getting a meal?
11. How do you think the girl felt while she was sitting on the fence telling her father about the squirrel?
12. What do you think was the father's reaction after he heard about the squirrel? How did he feel?
13. Why do you think the father said he had a present for the girl?

Episode 4

14. How do you think the girl felt when she *first* saw the calf?
15. Why do you think the father gave the girl a calf?
16. How do you think the father felt when he said to the girl the calf was her very own?
17. Why do you think the girl asked if the calf was born at the time she was killing the squirrel?
18. How do you think the boy felt while he was looking at the calf?

Episode 5

19. Why do you think the girl asked if she could feed the calf tonight?
20. Why do you think the boy said if he had a calf it would be bigger than the girl's?
21. How do you think the girl felt when she said, "But Pa didn't say it was just pretend"?
22. How do you think the father felt when he said maybe the mother was right and they ought to figure it that way?
23. Why do you suppose the mother changed her mind about the calf?
24. How do you think the girl felt when her mother said it might be a good thing for the girl to have something to take care of?
25. How do you think the boy felt when he said he wondered if the calf knew who it belonged to?

2. INSTRUCTIONS FOR CATEGORIZING ACCOUNTS

The child's complete account of what happened in an episode is to be considered as one unit. Read the response in its entirety and evaluate it as to the *presence or absence* of each of the categories below. For each category represented in the response, place a tally on the appropriate line of the categorization sheet. Any linguistic element which in and of itself is codable, and which if it appeared alone could be coded, is to be tallied. The categories fall within three main headings — reporting and describing, inferring and interpreting, and explaining. A given response may consist entirely of statements that report and describe; it may contain statements that report and describe and statements that infer and interpret; or it may include statements that report-describe, statements that infer-interpret, and statements that explain.

Reporting and Describing

The child may report on anything that she observed in the film. She may report her observations of the situation or the overt action, her observations of the verbal communication, her observations of expressive behavior. Or, she may describe feelings or intentions that are obviously presented in the dialogue, action, or expressive behavior. Such a statement would then be credited within the category of reporting-describing, and a tally placed on the line of the appropriate subheading.

Report of Situation-Action

Any empirical statement about the setting or external elements of a situation or about the beginning of a scene, any factual detail or any mention of a practical aspect is to be tallied within this category. For example, it was summer; the boy had a stick; the squirrel was dead; the boy was a guest; the father was sitting in a chair; they were driving home; they sat on the fence; the girl was skating; he was taking the girl to the circus; the bell rang.

Any empirical statement about the behavior or overt action of any of the actors is to be tallied within this category. For example, she was picking up the squirrel; they were washing their hands; the daddy showed her the calf; they were eating dinner; she put the skates over her shoulder; she went into the house.

Report of Verbal Communication

Any statement that repeats, paraphrases, or summarizes the content of the verbal communication of an actor is to be tallied within this category. For example, she was telling him about the squirrel; he said, "No, you can't"; they were talking about the calf.

If a child merely reports, "They were walking and talking," this would be categorized as reporting the situation-action. If the child reports, "They were walking and talking about what they were going to be," this would be categorized both as reporting the situation and reporting the verbal communication.

Report of Expressive Behavior

Any statement about the expressive behavior (i.e., the facial expression, gestures, or involuntary body movements) of an actor is to be tallied within this category. For example, she was crying; she was laughing; he was smiling; he was frowning.

Description of an Obvious Feeling

The child may make a statement that identifies or names a feeling. This may be simply in terms of a pleasant-positive feeling-tone or an unpleasant-negative feeling-tone. If the feeling was specifically mentioned in the dialogue of the film or was obviously manifested by the expressive behavior or by the action, the statement is to be tallied within this category. (Otherwise, a more subtle feeling or a complex feeling is to be tallied below in the category "inference of subtle feeling.") For example, the girl said she was happy; she felt good, he felt bad; she is crying, she feels sad; he is not sad; she told her father she was sorry.

Description of an Obvious Intention

The child may mention an intention, desire, purpose, wish or aim on the basis of her observations of the actor's action or verbal communication. If the intention was specifically mentioned in the dialogue of the film or was obviously manifested by the action, the statement is to be tallied within this category. (Otherwise, a more subtle intention is to be tallied below in the category of "inference of subtle intention.") For example, the boy said he wanted to skate; the girl didn't want the boy to have the skates.

Inferring or Interpreting

From her observation of the situation, the verbal communication, and the expressive behavior, the child may make an inference or an interpretation about the actor's subtle feelings, subtle intentions, thoughts, expectations, or interpersonal perceptions. Such a statement would then be credited within the category of inferring-interpreting, and a tally placed on the line of the appropriate subheading.

Inference of Subtle Feeling

If the child reports a feeling mentioned in the dialogue and does not comment on this or go beyond it, the statement would be tallied in the category above, "Description of an Obvious Feeling." If the child goes geyond the dialogue and expressive behavior, it would be tallied under "Inference of Subtle Feeling." Any combination of feelings that involves mixed feelings, including anxiety-producing conflict, would be categorized as "Inference of Subtle Feeling." For example, he felt jealous; she felt hurt; she felt disappointed, hurt, and bewildered; he felt surprised, annoyed, and angry.

Inference of Subtle Intention

Any inference of an anticipated action not explicitly mentioned in the film would be tallied within this category. For example, she was going to tell her father about what had happened. Any inference of an intention that is not specifically mentioned in the dialogue or obviously manifested by the action would be tallied within this category. These may be in terms of a person intending to create, arouse or obtain certain feelings in himself or in another; to avoid or relieve certain feelings in himself or in another; to accomplish certain effects; to communicate or express certain feelings; to obtain a specific object or to engage in a specific activity; to create certain thoughts, ideas, expectations or impressions. For example, he didn't want her to think he had to pay for it; she wanted to show him how she would do it.

Inference of Thought or Expectation

Any attribution of thoughts or expectations to an actor on the basis of the child's observations of the actor's actions, verbal communication, and expressive behavior would be tallied within this category. For example, she thought it was pretend; she thought it wouldn't hit him; she thought her mother was unfair; she expected him to side with her.

Inference of Interpersonal Perception

Any attribution of an interpersonal perception to an actor on the basis of the child's observations of the actor's actions, verbal communication, and expressive behavior would be tallied within this category. For example, he saw that she was happy; the mother saw from the girl's sad face that she had not said the right thing.

Explaining

The child may make a statement trying to account for the overt action, verbal communication, and expressive behavior she observed, or trying to account for the feelings, desires-intentions-purposes, thoughts-expectations-perceptions she interpreted. Any attempts to connect a situation with an action or feeling, two or more separate actions, two interpretations, or a reported action and an interpretation, would be credited as explaining and a tally placed on the line of the appropriate subheading. Any designation of sequential behavior would be considered a causal explanation. In general an explanation would include "because," "so," or some other connective. An explanation should *not* be inferred, but only credited if explicitly set forth by the child. If a child states, "The girl was crying and she was unhappy," this would be categorized as reporting the expressive behavior and describing an obvious feeling, but it would *not* be categorized as explaining the expressive behavior in terms of the feeling. A statement of a child might include reporting, interpreting, and explaining. For example, he sat down with her because he thought she felt sad.

71

In Situational Terms

If the child tries to account for her observations or interpretations in terms of the objective situation, the overt action of an actor, or the verbal communication of an actor, this would be categorized as explaining in situational terms. For example, she was sad because the squirrel was dead; she knocked him down because he said he was going to tell; he gave her the calf because he had a lot of calves; he rang the bell because he was the guest; she was happy because the calf was going to be hers; she felt sad because her mommy said she couldn't have it.

In Psychological Terms

If the child tries to explain the action, verbal communication, expressive behavior, feelings, or intentions of an actor in terms of the actor's own feelings, thoughts, expectations, or intentions, the statement would be tallied in this category of "explaining in psychological terms." For example, he wanted to do something for her because he felt sorry for her; he wanted to take her to the circus because he wanted to make up for what he had done; the father thought he had to punish the girl because the mother expected him to do it; she was sad because she thought her father didn't love her; she felt bad because she thought she wouldn't have anything to take care of; she felt good to get the calf because she wanted a pet.

In Terms of Interpersonal Perceptions

If the child tries to explain the action, verbal communication, expressive behavior, feelings, intentions, thoughts, in terms of an actor's interpersonal perceptions, the statement would be tallied in this category. For example, the mother changed her mind because she saw how sad her daughter felt; he offered her a ride on the elephant because he saw how thrilled she was with the tricks; the father gave her the calf because he saw she was so unhappy about the squirrel.

3. STATISTICAL METHODS

In order to determine the statistical significance of comparisons between age groups, it was decided to use a confidence coefficient of .95, and the confidence intervals for a sample of 20 children were obtained from *Biometrika Tables for Statisticians*.[1] This table is reproduced on page 73.

---

[1] E. S. Pearson and H. O. Hartley (eds.), *Biometrika tables for statisticians*, Vol. I (Cambridge: Cambridge Univ. Press, 1954), Table 41, p. 204.

NINETY-FIVE PERCENT CONFIDENCE INTERVALS FOR P

N = 20

Observed number	Confidence interval
0	0 — .21
1	0 — .25
2	.01 — .32
3	.03 — .38
4	.06 — .44
5	.09 — .49
6	.12 — .54
7	.15 — .59
8	.19 — .64
9	.23 — .68
10	.27 — .73
11	.32 — .77
12	.36 — .81
13	.41 — .85
14	.46 — .88
15	.51 — .91
16	.56 — .94
17	.62 — .97
18	.68 — .99
19	.75 — 1.00
20	.79 — 1.00

Differences between age groups were considered significant only where there was no overlap between the 95 percent confidence intervals of the two observed numbers. For example, if 10 six-year-olds in the sample made statements classified within a given category, the observed proportion in this category was .50 (i.e., 10/20). According to the table, the 95 percent confidence interval for this observed number of 10 is .27–.73. In other words, it could be said that the degree of confidence is .95 that the proportion of six-year-olds in the population who would make statements that would be classified within the same category is between .27 and .73. Examining the table to see which other observed numbers do *not* have confidence intervals that overlap with that for 10, it can be seen that the confidence interval for 19 is .75–1.00. That is, it could be said that if 19 twelve-year-olds in the sample made statements classified within the same category, giving an observed proportion of .95 (i.e., 19/20), there is confidence .95 that the proportion of twelve-year-olds in the population who would make statements in this category is between .75 and 1.00. Since there is no overlap between the 95 percent confidence interval of .27–.73 for an observed number of 10 six-year-olds and the 95 percent confidence interval of .75–1.00 for an observed number of 19 twelve-year-olds, it can be stated that the difference between the six-year-olds and the twelve-year-olds is statistically significant.

TABLE 7

Categorization of the Children's Statements about What Happened in the Movies:
Agreement between Two Judges

(Based on responses of 7 children in each age group)

Categories of statements	Six-year-olds			Nine-year-olds			Twelve-year-olds		
	Number of statements	Number of agreements	Percent agreement	Number of statements	Number of agreements	Percent agreement	Number of statements	Number of agreements	Percent agreement
Reporting and describing									
Situation-action	264	264	100	394	394	100	374	374	100
Verbal communication	258	258	100	652	652	100	507	507	100
Expressive behavior	22	22	100	29	29	100	19	19	100
Obvious feelings	27	27	100	56	56	100	46	46	100
Obvious intentions	20	19	95	44	44	100	44	43	98
Interpreting and inferring									
Feelings	—	—	—	12	11	92	15	14	93
Thoughts-expectations	7	6	86	29	27	93	19	17	90
Intentions-motives	5	4	80	6	5	83	11	10	91
Interpersonal perceptions	—	—	—	6	6	100	4	4	100
Explaining									
In situational terms	10	9	90	25	24	96	17	16	94
In psychological terms	9	8	89	16	15	94	10	9	90
In terms of interpersonal perceptions	—	—	—	6	5	83	4	4	100
All statements	622	617	99	1275	1268	99	1070	1063	99

TABLE 8

Categorization of the Children's Statements about What Happened in the Movie:
Agreement between Two Categorizations, One Week Apart, by One Judge

(Based on responses of 20 children in each age group)

Categories of statements	Six-year-olds			Nine-year-olds			Twelve-year-olds		
	Number of statements	Number of agreements	Percent agreement	Number of statements	Number of agreements	Percent agreement	Number of statements	Number of agreements	Percent agreement
Reporting and describing									
Situation-action	778	770	99	1092	1080	99	1039	1029	99
Verbal communication	717	715	100	1694	1690	100	1570	1565	100
Expressive behavior	45	44	100	46	46	100	54	54	100
Obvious feelings	71	71	100	89	89	100	136	136	100
Obvious intentions	31	29	94	114	110	97	113	110	97
Interpreting and inferring									
Feelings	–	–	–	37	35	95	57	54	95
Thoughts-expectations	7	6	86	41	38	93	61	59	97
Intentions-motives	5	4	80	12	11	92	32	30	94
Interpersonal perceptions	–	–	–	6	6	100	11	11	100
Explaining									
In situational terms	33	30	91	82	76	93	76	70	92
In psychological terms	9	8	89	30	27	90	33	30	91
In terms of interpersonal perceptions	–	–	–	7	7	100	10	10	100
All statements	1696	1677	99	3250	3215	99	3192	3158	99

TABLE 9

Agreement between Judges in Assigning Scores of 0, 1, or 2 to Responses to Interview Questions

	Six-year-olds			Nine-year-olds			Twelve-year-olds		
	Number of items	Number of agreements	Percent agreement	Number of items	Number of agreements	Percent agreement	Number of items	Number of agreements	Percent agreement
Movie A[a]	40	37	93	40	35	88	40	36	90
0	13	13	100	5	5	100	1	1	100
1	23	21	91	21	19	91	15	14	93
2	4	3	75	14	11	79	24	21	88
Movie B[a]	40	37	93	40	37	93	40	38	95
0	17	17	100	7	7	100	4	4	100
1	19	17	90	22	20	91	17	16	94
2	4	3	75	11	10	91	19	18	95

[a] Two items chosen at random from the protocols of each of the twenty children at each age level.

TABLE 10

Agreement between Scorings, One Week Apart, by One Judge, in Assigning Scores of 0, 1, or 2 to Responses to Interview Questions

	Six-year-olds			Nine-year-olds			Twelve-year-olds		
	Number of items	Number of agreements	Percent agreement	Number of items	Number of agreements	Percent agreement	Number of items	Number of agreements	Percent agreement
Movie A[a]	560	532	95	560	534	95	560	537	96
0	191	188	98	73	72	99	41	40	98
1	323	305	95	306	291	95	230	222	97
2	46	39	85	181	171	95	289	275	95
Movie B[b]	500	477	95	500	478	96	500	487	97
0	223	219	98	89	88	99	58	57	98
1	241	229	95	272	259	95	220	215	98
2	36	29	81	139	131	94	222	215	97

[a] Twenty children at each age responded to twenty-eight questions.
[b] Twenty children at each age responded to twenty-five questions.

TABLE 11

Number of Children at Each Age Level Whose Answers Were Scored 0, 1, or 2 on the Interview Questions of Movie A and Movie B

(N at each age is 20)

Questions asked	Number of answers of six-year-olds scored			Number of answers of nine-year-olds scored			Number of answers of twelve-year-olds scored		
	0	1	2	0	1	2	0	1	2
Episode 1									
1. Why do you think the boy called the girl a pig?	2	17	1	0	16	4	1	15	4
2. How do you think the mother felt when she looked out the window and said to let the boy have the skates?	6	14	0	1	13	6	0	9	11
3. Why do you think the girl pushed the boy down?	7	13	0	3	14	3	2	15	3
Episode 2									
4. When the father and mother were talking together, why do you think the father said his hand was too big?	6	14	0	4	13	3	1	13	6
5. Why do you think the mother said she was busy making supper?	11	6	3	1	14	5	1	15	4
6. How do you think the girl felt when the boy lied and said he didn't call her a pig?	6	14	0	2	12	6	2	12	6
7. How do you think the girl felt when she took off the skates and said she was going to bed without any supper?	9	11	0	9	7	4	4	4	12
8. Why do you think the father gave the skates to the boy?	5	13	2	1	15	4	0	11	9

	Question									
9.	How do you think the girl felt after the father gave the skates to the boy?	0	19	1	1	15	4	0	5	15
10.	How do you think the father felt after he gave the skates to the boy and after the girl went into the house?	9	10	1	5	11	4	6	6	8
11.	How do you think the boy felt after the father gave him the skates?	3	17	0	2	13	5	2	10	8

Episode 3

	Question									
12.	At the beginning, why do you think the father kept looking up instead of reading the newspaper?	13	2	5	8	4	8	6	3	11
13.	Why do you think the girl asked to kiss her father good night?	5	10	5	3	10	7	0	5	15
14.	How do you think the father felt when the girl asked to kiss him good night?	8	12	0	1	7	12	1	4	15
15.	Why do you think the father said he was going to take a bath?	12	6	2	5	9	6	1	10	9
16.	Why do you think the mother mentioned the circus to the father?	14	0	6	3	0	17	1	0	19
17.	How do you think the father felt after the mother mentioned the circus?	10	10	0	3	5	12	0	5	15

Episode 4

	Question									
18.	Why do you think the father asked the driver to take the elephant out of the truck?	3	12	5	0	4	16	0	1	19
19.	Why do you think the father told his daughter the driver was always glad to show elephants to little girls?	13	5	2	1	9	10	0	4	16
20.	Why do you think the man asked the girl if she would like to take a ride on the elephant?	8	9	3	4	3	13	0	2	18

TABLE 11 (Continued)

Number of Children at Each Age Level Whose Answers Were Scored 0, 1, or 2 on the Interview Questions of Movie A and Movie B

(N at each age is 20)

Questions asked	Number of answers of six-year-olds scored			Number of answers of nine-year-olds scored			Number of answers of twelve-year-olds scored		
	0	1	2	0	1	2	0	1	2
21. How do you think the girl felt while she was on the elephant?	3	17	0	0	16	4	0	7	13
22. How do you think the father felt while the girl was on the elephant?	4	15	1	0	17	3	0	13	7
Episode 5									
23. How do you think the girl felt as she and her father were driving home?	3	17	0	0	16	4	0	13	7
24. Why do you think the girl felt happy?	1	17	2	0	14	6	0	11	9
25. Why do you think the girl asked if she could kiss her father good night this time?	3	11	6	0	14	6	1	7	12
26. How do you think the father felt as they were driving home?	1	19	0	1	14	5	1	9	10
27. Why do you think the father felt happy?	8	11	1	1	16	3	0	16	4
28. Why do you think the father said there would be more nice things happening to her?	18	2	0	14	5	1	11	5	4
Totals	191	323	46	73	306	181	41	230	289

TABLE 12

Number of Children at Each Age Level Whose Answers Were Scored 0, 1, or 2 on the Interview Questions of Movie B

(N at each age is 20)

Questions asked	Number of answers of six-year-olds scored			Number of answers of nine-year-olds scored			Number of answers of twelve-year-olds scored		
	0	1	2	0	1	2	0	1	2
Episode 1									
1. Why do you think the boy said his father killed all the buffalo?	16	1	3	9	5	6	7	4	9
2. Why do you think the girl threw the rock?	10	6	4	1	8	11	1	11	8
3. How do you think the girl felt after she threw the rock?	1	19	0	0	15	5	0	13	7
4. Why do you think the girl cried after the rock hit the squirrel?	2	12	6	2	6	12	0	3	17
5. Why do you think the boy said red squirrels are bad?	18	0	2	8	3	9	9	2	9
Episode 2									
6. How do you think the girl felt about the boy ringing the dinner bell?	6	13	1	2	13	5	1	3	16
7. How do you think the girl felt when her mother told her to wash her face?	10	10	0	5	14	1	1	17	2
8. How do you think the mother felt after the girl said she didn't touch anything with her face?	16	3	1	6	12	2	3	13	4

TABLE 12 (Continued)

Number of Children at Each Age Level Whose Answers Were Scored 0, 1, or 2 on the Interview Questions of Movie B

(N at each age is 20)

Questions asked	Number of answers of six-year-olds scored			Number of answers of nine-year-olds scored			Number of answers of twelve-year-olds scored		
	0	1	2	0	1	2	0	1	2
Episode 3									
9. Why do you think the girl talked about squirrels being bad?	11	8	1	2	14	4	0	5	15
10. Why do you think the father asked, "What's the matter?" after he said he didn't mind the squirrels getting a meal?	9	9	2	0	11	9	2	13	5
11. How do you think the girl felt while she was sitting on the fence telling her father about the squirrel?	0	20	0	4	15	1	1	11	8
12. What do you think was the father's reaction after he heard about the squirrel? How did he feel?	3	16	1	2	10	8	2	9	9
13. Why do you think the father said he had a present for the girl?	13	7	0	3	9	8	3	9	8
Episode 4									
14. How do you think the girl felt when she *first* saw the calf?	0	20	0	0	18	2	0	17	3

Question									
15. Why do you think the father gave the girl a calf?	16	3	1	10	5	5	11	2	7
16. How do you think the father felt when he said to the girl the calf was her very own?	4	16	0	1	17	2	2	14	4
17. Why do you think the girl asked if the calf was born at the time she was killing the squirrel?	17	3	0	2	12	6	5	1	14
18. How do you think the boy felt while he was looking at the calf?	15	3	2	11	7	2	3	11	6
Episode 5									
19. Why do you think the girl asked if she could feed the calf tonight?	8	12	0	0	20	0	2	14	4
20. Why do you think the boy said if he had a calf it would be bigger than the girl's?	15	2	3	2	7	11	1	5	14
21. How do you think the girl felt when she said, "But Pa didn't said it was just pretend"?	2	18	0	1	15	4	0	10	10
22. How do you think the father felt when he said maybe the mother was right and they ought to figure it that way?	4	15	1	5	10	5	2	4	14
23. Why do you suppose the mother changed her mind about the calf?	7	5	8	2	4	14	1	1	18
24. How do you think the girl felt when her mother said it might be a good thing for the girl to have something to take care of?	4	16	0	2	16	2	0	18	2
25. How do you think the boy felt when he said he wondered if the calf knew who it belonged to?	16	4	0	9	6	5	1	10	9
Totals	223	241	36	89	272	139	58	220	222

Bibliography

AMEN, ELIZABETH W. "Individual differences in apperceptive reaction: A study of the responses of preschool children to pictures," *Genet. Psychol. Monogr.*, XXIII (1941), 319–85.

ANSBACHER, HEINZ and ANSBACHER, ROWENA R. *The individual psychology of Alfred Adler.* New York: Basic Books, 1956. 503 pp.

AUSUBEL, DAVID P. "Socioempathy as a function of sociometric status in an adolescent group," *Human Relat.*, VIII (1955), 75–84.

———. *Theory and problems of child development.* New York: Grune and Stratton, 1958. 650 pp.

AUSUBEL, DAVID P. and SCHIFF, HERBERT M. "Some intrapersonal and interpersonal determinants of individual differences in sociempathic ability among adolescents," *J. Soc. Psychol.*, XLI (1955), 39–56.

AUSUBEL, DAVID P., SCHIFF, HERBERT M., and GASSER, EDWARD B. "A preliminary study of developmental trends in sociempathy: Accuracy of perception of own and others' sociometric status," *Child Develpm.*, XXIII (1952), 111–28.

BATHURST, J. E. "A study of sympathy and resistance (negativism) among children," *Psychol. Bull.*, XXX (1933), 625–26.

BURNS, NEAL and CAVEY, LORNA. "Age differences in empathic ability among children," *Canad. J. Psychol.*, XI (1957), 227–30.

COOLEY, CHARLES H. *Sociological theory and social research.* New York: Henry Holt, 1930. 345 pp.

DAVITZ, JOEL R. "Social perception and sociometric choice of children," *J. Abnorm. Soc. Psychol.*, L (1955), 173–76.

DYMOND, ROSALIND F., HUGHES, ANNE S., and RAABE, VIRGINIA L.

"Measurable changes in empathy with age," *J. Consult. Psychol.* XVI (1952), 202–206.

ESTVAN, FRANK J., and ESTVAN, ELIZABETH W. *The child's world: His social perception.* New York: G. P. Putnam's Sons, 1959. 302 pp.

FOOTE, NELSON N. and COTTRELL, LEONARD S., JR. *Identity and interpersonal competence: A new direction in family research.* Chicago: Univ. of Chicago Press, 1955. 305 pp.

GATES, GEORGINA STRICKLAND. "An experimental study of the growth of social perception," *J. Educ. Psychol.*, XIV (1923), 449–61.

GIBBONS, CHARLES C. and PORTER, JAMES P. "Some aspects of social adaptability among adolescents," *J. Appl. Psychol.*, XXIII (1939), 508–20.

GIBSON, JAMES J. "Social psychology and the psychology of perceptual learning." In M. Sherif and M. O. Wilson (eds.), *Group relations at the crossroads.* New York: Harper, 1958. 379 pp.

GOLLIN, EUGENE S. "Organizational characteristics of social judgments: A developmental investigation," *J. Pers.*, XXVI (1958), 139–54.

HARRIS, ESTHER KITE. "The responsiveness of kindergarten children to the behavior of their fellows," *Monogr. Soc. Res. Child Developm.*, XI (1946), No. 2. 184 pp.

HSIA, JUI-CHING. *A study of the sociability of elementary school children.* Contributions to Education, No. 322. New York: Bureau of Publications. Teachers College, Columbia Univ., 1928. 64 pp.

INHELDER, BARBEL and PIAGET, JEAN. *The growth of logical thinking from childhood to adolescence.* New York: Basic Books, 1958. 356 pp.

JERSILD, ARTHUR T. "Self-understanding in childhood and adolescence," *Amer. Psychologist,* VI (1951), 122–26.

MILLER, ROBERT V. "Social status and socioempathic differences," *Except. Child.*, XXIII (1956), 114–19.

MURPHY, LOIS B. *Social behavior and child personality.* New York: Columbia Univ. Press, 1937. 344 pp.

OJEMANN, RALPH H., *et al.* "The effects of a 'causal' teacher-training program and certain curricular changes on grade school children," *J. Exp. Educ.*, XXIV (1955), 95–114.

PEARSON, E. S. and HARTLEY, H. O. (eds.). *Biometrika tables for statisticians.* Vol. I. Cambridge: Cambridge Univ. Press, 1954. 238 pp.

PIAGET, JEAN. *Judgment and reasoning in the child.* New York: Harcourt, Brace, 1928. 260 pp.

———. *The language and thought of the child.* (3rd ed.) New York: Humanities Press, 1959. 288 pp.

———. *The moral judgment of the child.* Glencoe: Free Press, 1960. 418 pp.

Russell, David H. *Children's thinking.* Boston: Ginn, 1956. 449 pp.

Walton, William E. "Empathic responses in children," *Psychol. Monogr.*, XLVIII (1936), 40–67.

Winch, William H. "Children's perceptions," *Educ. Psychol. Monogr.* (Baltimore: Warwich and York), 1914. No. 12. 245 pp.

Yarrow, Marian Radke and Campbell, John D. "Person perception in children," *Merrill-Palmer Quart.*, IX (1963), 57–72.